DEVON'S
FIFTY BEST
CHURCHES

A PERSONAL CHOICE

DEVON'S
FIFTY BEST
CHURCHES
A PERSONAL CHOICE

TODD GRAY

THE MINT PRESS

The Mint Press
Taddyforde House South,
Taddyforde Estate,
New North Road,
Exeter EX4 4AT

British Library Cataloguing in Publication Data
Data available

Cover, text design and page make-up by Delphine Jones, Exeter, England
Printed in Great Britain by Short Run Press, Exeter, England

ISBN 978 1 903356 60 9

CONTENTS

THE FIFTY

ACKNOWLEDGMENTS

I am deeply grateful to friends and colleagues with whom I have crisscrossed more than 8,000 miles through every part of Devon on church crawls and would like to thank John Allan, Michael Clayson, David Cook, Judith Cosford, Carole & Ray Herbert, Meg Hitchcock, Martin & Rosemary Horrell, Laurence Hunt, David Kremer, Willow MacFarlan, Olive Millward, Richard Parker, Mark Rowe, Bob Vicary, Rob Ward and Keith Stevens for their time, interest and patience. Churchwardens and officers have shared their knowledge and opened their churches to allow me access. I am very grateful to them for the many kindnesses they have shown. I am also indebted to the staff, too many to name individually, of the Devon Record Office, North Devon Athenaeum, North Devon Record Office, Plymouth & West Devon Record Office, Plymouth Local Studies Library, University of Exeter Main Library and Westcountry Studies Library. I would also like to thank Delphine Jones for her superb cover. David Cook, Steve Hobbs, Emeritus Professor Christopher Holdsworth, Bill Jerman, Dr Neil Rushton and Thomasin Westcott have been generous in answering questions. I am particularly grateful to John Allan for his suggestions in improving the text: he has been supportive from the start and I have benefited greatly from his deep knowledge of Devon. Richard Parker has also been generous with his time and with sharing his expertise. I also owe him a great debt. Any and all mistakes are of course my own.

NOTE

The first Devon church that I visited was in Plymouth. I was then a young lad being shown Charles church as a second-world war bomb site. The layers of history, still visible despite the destruction, fascinated me. Over the succeeding forty years I have managed to visit each of the county's 475 ancient parish churches at least once and most of the remaining 150 or so more modern ones.

The structures in themselves are fascinating but the richness of the fittings is a joy which I hope anyone who is unfamiliar with will find as rewarding as I do. This book is, by its very nature, a personal choice and there will be many who will disagree with me on ones which I have included as well as those which I have left out. It will hopefully stir up interest and debate on churches in general and result in visits to these and other buildings. Each and every church in Devon has something to offer and many are rich in various and wonderful ways. No Nonconformist church or chapel have been included because these buildings lack the layers of history the Anglican churches retain. Exeter Cathedral was also excluded from the outset because it dwarfs all other churches in so many different ways. I have based my choices mostly on which churches have outstanding fabric but also partly on the overall effect the building produces, on what is commonly called the 'wow factor'. I hope that each of these buildings results in a satisfying visit although I appreciate that tastes differ and not everyone enjoys the Arts & Crafts movement equally as they do Victorian Gothic or the Elizabethan period or vice versa. Even so, each of these 50 buildings have extraordinary treasures to enjoy that will enrich a visitor's life.

Todd Gray
Taddyforde, September 2011

FOREWORD

Devon's churches have been one of the most noticeable and constant features of the landscape for a thousand years. These buildings and their fabric are a testament to the practice of faith over these centuries, yet have also changed as the ways in which we worship have changed. Each generation has left their mark and the result is that in Devon we have a rich legacy of historical and human interest. We can easily take it for granted and perhaps too few of us travel across the county to see just how much there is in all of our parish churches.

Devon's Fifty Best Churches reminds us of what is there to be discovered and valued. It encapsulates the best in the measured opinion of one of our county's leading and best known historians. However, in addition to the churches described here, there are more than another 500 in the Diocese of Exeter to be enjoyed, understood and cherished. Church Tourism is very much on our agenda now, and the congregations in these 50 churches will warmly welcome visitors who are embarking on what are now commonly known as 'church crawls'.

I warmly recommend this book.

+ Michael Exon:

The Right Reverend Michael Langrish
Bishop of Exeter

Dartington Church

INTRODUCTION

ollectively Devon's Anglican churches form the county's greatest storehouse of our ancient treasures. They house items of extraordinary beauty and showcase the work of thousands of men and women, many of whom would be otherwise forgotten. Even so, it has not been by intent that these churches have become Devon's greatest museum of art. The buildings were built as centres of faith and devotion and continue to fulfil that purpose. Nevertheless, in them are extraordinary objects. Who could fail to be intrigued by the three-faced 'pumpkin head' at **Winkleigh*** or be surprised by the cheeky behaviour of the mischievous lads at Offwell who, carved in stone, flash their bottoms at each other? The gingerbread men on the Norman font at Spreyton are pleasingly primitive, the medieval Devonians at **Doddiscombsleigh** continue to peer into the church five centuries after they were first painted in glass and the seventeenth-century slate image of a mother with her infant memorialised at Monkleigh still conveys great sadness and sorrow.

Nevertheless, there are few individuals today who have managed to see the best that there is, let alone visit every Anglican church in Devon. The sheer number of buildings, there are more than 600, and the geographical size of the county, the second largest in the country, are largely responsible for the public's unawareness of the great wealth of riches hidden about them. The fault also lies with insufficient guidance in the way of research and publications. Many items have been poorly researched and despite a number of publications most visitors remain unsure of how to choose the most interesting or rewarding buildings that Devon has to offer. It is the intention of this book to highlight those churches which should not be missed.

A thousand years and more of religious practice have left us with a splendid heritage but the extent of it can make visiting a building confusing and overwhelming. One useful step when approaching a church is to note the building materials. Many are made from local stone but there are remarkable exceptions such as George Nympton where the tower was built of brick in 1673 and many others have stone which was brought from considerable distances. In Devon the majority of the towers are situated at the west end of the church but some ten per cent lie elsewhere and it is interesting to note where these exceptions are.

* *The use of bold type indicates this church is one of the fifty.*

It is also worthwhile to assess if the churchyard has been reordered or whether the gravestones have been left where they were originally set.

Porches were mostly built on the south side, can be highly ornamental, like that at Chawleigh, and some are two-storied. Before entering the building it is rewarding to have a quick look at the windows themselves, occasionally they are made of wood, as at **Teigngrace**. From the outside it is generally possible to see easily if there are aisles and side chapels.

Most Devon churches have guides but it is useful to come prepared by looking at the listed building survey which is now online and available at the Westcountry Studies Library. From these it is possible to assess quickly if the building was given a Victorian or modern restoration or refurbishment. That is, was it a rebuilding or just a makeover? It is useful to also assess what type of congregation is now in the church. Questions to consider are whether it is high or low church and how the church is currently used. Most importantly, have the seats been recently reordered with a great change of the fabric?

These all help us to begin to understand what we are looking at. The history of the Anglican church is revealed through the fabric contained in the parish churches but great insights into local history can also be discovered in these buildings.

The Medieval Church

Little remains to be seen today of the earliest days of the Christian Church in Devon, the late 300s, but there is evidence of a steady evangelising over the following centuries by Irish, Welsh and Breton missionaries. In these years Devon was part of various and differently geographically-arranged dioceses. This lasted for nearly 350 years until 1050 when the See finally only comprised Devon and Cornwall and the bishop returned his seat to Exeter.

It is for this earlier period, the Saxon settlement of the county, that there can be discovered a decorated cross shaft in the church at **Colyton**, found embedded in the wall after a devastating fire in 1933, while at Dolton can be seen a font made up partly of another Saxon cross. Sidbury has a Saxon crypt and in Exeter there are architectural remains at **Sts. Martin**, George and Olave. Compared to other parts of England there is little to be found in Devon of the Saxons. Their original buildings are assumed to have been wooden and rebuilt by the Normans when they arrived in the late eleventh century. It is for these newcomers that their work can be discovered in a great number of churches.

The Normans

When the Normans arrived, in the 1060s, the Bishop of Exeter was the third greatest landowner in Devon; only the king and sheriff held more land. In the following century parish boundaries were being defined and their clerics carved out territory alongside the increasing number of religious houses being built in Devon.

The best known Norman towers are those at Exeter Cathedral which were begun in the 1100s and there may be some parish churches with Norman towers that later rebuilding and or enlargement have disguised. Some, like **Barnstaple**, have their tower walls hidden within the church at the centre of a cruciform plan where the arms of the cross meet. Others include Axminster, **Colyton**, **Crediton**, Shute and **Tawstock**. Perhaps Devon once had free-standing towers? There are some small inconspicuous Norman

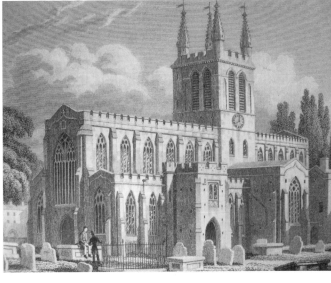

CREDITON

churches, for example Bickleigh chapel and a number in North West Devon, as well as some larger churches such as Upton Hellions and Highampton.

Norman doorways can also be found in all parts of Devon. At **Shebbear**, Buckland Brewer and Bishopsteignton there are the wonderfully barbaric Beakhead doorways. These have surprising details and seem to modern eyes to be more akin to South American art forms than those commonly associated with the Normans. More restrained Norman doorways can be discovered at Axminster and **Paignton**. Devon's great Norman surprise is the series of carvings found at **Hawkchurch**.

THE NORMAN FONT AT HARTLAND CHURCH

Inside Devon's churches there is also a wealth of Norman and later medieval fonts made from a great variety of stone including from Beer, Caen and Dartmoor. Although many are positioned near the south door this may not always have been so. More than a hundred survive in a variety of forms including those which resemble goblets, eggcups or like a squared capital. Others are like table tops. The decorations which are most striking feature heads of humans and other creatures (Bratton Clovelly, Braunton, Lifton, Stoodleigh). The font at **South Milton** should not be missed but the most extraordinary of all is that at Luppitt with its series of strange beings and scenes. St Marychurch is another highly interesting font as is that at Alphington with its hunting motif. Oddities include that at Stoke Canon where it may have been inspired by earlier art, that of the Celts, than of the continental Normans.

Gothic

A new style, Gothic, was taken up nationally in the early 1200s and is usually divided into three phases, the Early English, Decorated and Perpendicular. Devon has few examples of Early English work until the end of the 1300s. By this date the second stage was over and the third stage had overtaken architectural fashion.

AT WIDWORTHY CHURCH

The first phase, the Early English period, began the Gothic movement by introducing the innovations of pointed arches, ribbed vaulting and flying buttresses. It radically altered what new building that there was. Some details can be seen in East Devon at **Branscombe**, Farway and Colaton Raleigh. The ruins at Frithelstock Priory also have this detail. Little else survives which could indicate that little had been executed at this time in Devon.

The second phase, the Decorated Style, which was taken up at the end of the 1200s, is also poorly represented locally with Exeter Cathedral and **Ottery St Mary** being the more obvious exceptions. There are also features in the impressive churches of **Bere Ferrers** and **Haccombe** as well as smaller ones like Shaldon and those with aisled naves such as Ugborough, Diptford and Staverton. In parish churches the style is most noticeable in the towers and spires in two areas focused around Barnstaple and Kingsbridge. In regards to monuments the most conspicuous work is also at Exeter Cathedral and **Ottery St Mary** but there are also good memorials at such places as **Atherington**, **Bere Ferrers**, Membury and **Mortehoe**.

These are patchy survivals of the two early styles in comparison to the majority of Devon churches which can be seen to have been developed with the third phase, the Perpendicular Style. This began in the late 1300s at Exeter Cathedral and mostly from the early 1400s in the rest of the county. In the late 1700s Reverend Polwhele, one of Devon's first historians, concluded that little had been done up to the early fourteenth century. He noted:

> 'the inferior houses in Devon and Cornwall were built with mud, which was called cob, that our superior fabrics were constructed chiefly of schist and freestone in the east and marble in other parts of Devon – that our churches, consisting of the same materials, were erected from the year 1300 to 1550.'

16

ABOVE: Haccombe
Top Middle: Bere Ferrers
Top right: Tamerton Foliot
middle left: Atherington
Middle right: Ottery St Mary
Below left: Haccombe
Below right: Bere Ferrers

This third period can be found in nearly every Devon church and could have obliterated earlier building features. Some outstanding work can be seen at **Cullompton**, **Ottery St Mary** and **Tiverton** and is largely associated with the increased wealth brought to Devon through the woollen cloth trade. The latter's south porch and chapel was built in 1517 by John Greenway who appears kneeling at the Assumption of the Virgin, a great achievement for a local cloth merchant.

By this time Devon had experienced the Black Death and recovered. By 1348, when the Black Death began to strike, Devon had thousands of new farms carved out of the land, salt-water marshes had been drained and heath-land had been converted to pasture or for the plough. The county is thought to have suffered particularly badly from the disease and in Exeter as much as a third of the population, if not more, died in the first outbreak. Yet Devon had strongly recovered in the early 1400s. Perhaps the loss of population had turned farms from arable to pasture which increased the production of wool for cloth.

In every corner of Devon parish churches were extended with new aisles being added to either side of the nave, nearly always of comparable height, right to the end of chancel. The result was the creation of two new chapels and the exterior appearance of three parallel gables and three windows at the east end.

Devon's churches are distinguished in this period by three forms of woodwork. The one which can be easily missed is the roof which takes the craning of one's neck to appreciate properly. Binoculars are a great help. The roofs are often unbroken; they stretch through the nave and into the chancel. Known variously as cradle, wagon or barrel roofs, they are often ceiled and ornamented with rich carvings.

The second wooden feature is the bench with its carved end. More survive in North Devon than in the south, with **East Budleigh** the notable exception, and nearly all of them date from the early 1500s. They generally have rectangular ends with some motifs being initials, presumably of benefactors, as well as heraldic shields and coats of arms, figures of saints, symbols

ONE OF EAST BUDLEIGH'S GREAT BENCHENDS

of the Passion and grotesques of all shapes and sizes. These benches continued to be inserted into churches through the sixteenth century and took on new forms but there are also many churches with very plain unadorned benches such as **Parracombe**.

Devon's greatest wooden treasures are its screens. It has nearly 150. They have been described as dazzling. It remains a puzzle as to why so many survive compared to the rest of England. Instructions from the bishop may have been a factor. Another may have been that during the Reformist years, particularly from the 1530s through to the 1570s, Devon men and women were reluctant to destroy items that had been expensive to install and largely devoid of carved images of saints. No doubt this was helped by the confusing flip-flop of the crown's religious directions from Catholic Henry VIII's leanings to Protestantism in the 1530s to his daughter Mary's revival of Catholicism in 1553 and finally to the return of the Protestant church under Elizabeth five years later. Perhaps this religious uncertainty, continued into and through to the end of the 1600s with the suspected Catholicism of King Charles, the civil wars of the middle of the century and the anxiety caused by the melodramas of the 1680s with King James and then William of Orange, led many Devonians to largely sit tight in their rural isolated parish churches. It would have been sensible to be cautious.

The screens symbolised the veil between earth and heaven and emphasised the sanctity of the chancel. The figures on the screen comprised carvings of those of the crucifixion on top of the screen (the rood) as well as carved and painted saints and angels throughout the screen. They represented the heavenly host which

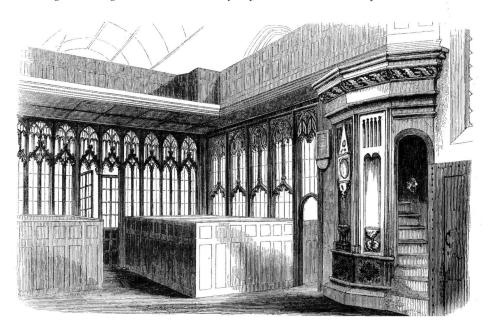

TOTNES

assisted passage to paradise. During services communicants passed through the screen, and thus the holy figures, to encounter God. Only **Atherington** still has the rood loft, a survival from the early 1500s. Perhaps the concession that many Devonians made during religious pressure was merely to remove the rood loft itself as an idolatrous object but keep their less objectionable screens which could have unacceptable images painted over or removed.

Whatever reasoning these Devonians may have had, they have left us an impressive range of wood carving. The lights can be separated by varying widths of mullions but the observer is more likely to first notice the rich coving above with all manner of decoration. Three local types of screens have been identified with one at **Dartmouth** and to the parishes to the west, another dispersed in the South Hams and a third in mid Devon around Coldridge. The carved portraits at Morchard Bishop are particularly engaging.

The carvers of some screens have been identified as local men. We can see at **Atherington** the work of men from Northlew and Chittlehampton. Roger Down and John Hyll of the latter parish completed the screen for £14 7s 7d in the 1540s.

Another aspect of the screens that instantly attracts the eye is the panelling beneath the carved lights. A few have carved figures (notably Bridford), others with later ornament (South Pool) but the most common are the painted figures often of saints and biblical figures (**Ashton**). One of the most appealing is at Buckland in the Moor which has defaced images of the Nativity.

Screens were also carved of stone with the most decorated, not surprisingly, being found at Exeter Cathedral and **Ottery St Mary**. The design was copied at **Totnes** and at **Colyton**. Other stone screens can be found at **Awliscombe**, Dunsford and Marldon. The Gothic pulpits were often carved of stone with figures of saints (**Swimbridge**, Dittisham and particularly North Molton).

Not surprisingly, it is Exeter Cathedral that is known for its stained glass but perhaps more rewarding is a visit to **Doddiscombsleigh** which has the astounding seven sacraments glass. It can also be seen much more easily. **Littlehempston** has fifteenth-century images of Saints Stephen and Christopher. Below them are two couples at prayer with one of the women clutching her rosary beads. Bampton also has a fascinating medieval glass window, the fragments taken from an existing window, moved and then pieced together as a Great War memorial. More interesting is that at Calverleigh where the glass came from France in 1887. The rest of Devon's medieval glass is fragmentary. Other good glass can be found at Awliscombe with its gaunt figure on crutches, one of several which had formerly been in a chapel but later removed from the church and then returned. Bridford's fragments include a monster sticking his tongue out, a motif found in churches throughout Devon.

Monuments are exceptionally good at Exeter Cathedral but there is another in Exeter at St Mary Arches as well as at **Atherington**, where the two effigies have good faces. Even better are those at **Littlehempston** and **Tamerton Foliot**.

20

The Reformation from the 1530s to the Glorious Revolution

We can only guess at how much destruction was initiated by the introduction of Protestantism. Most objects were poorly recorded and are thus completely lost to us. Some items were quietly destroyed while others were lost in a very public manner such as on a great bonfire in Exeter's Cathedral Close in 1559. The accounts of the vicar at Morebath, one of Devon's most important records, show items were sold but others were quietly distributed amongst local farmers in 1548. They, a few years later, returned objects to the church 'like true and faithful Christian people'. Morebath waited to do this until Queen Mary was on the throne. The side altar was rededicated and the rood was put up again but it was only a few short years later, with the coronation of Elizabeth, that the changes were reversed.

The church at Morebath today bears no trace of this devious concealment and attempted preservation.

THE CHAPEL AT PAIGNTON CHURCH

It would be easy to presume that this happened across Devon but as times changed it is likely that rescuers' descendants quietly destroyed any troublesome artefacts or they deteriorated on their own. Even so, we can find on Devon bench-ends the five wounds of Christ, the emblem used on the flag of the Prayer Book rebels who swept through Devon from Sampford Courtenay in 1549. The importance of these symbols can be seen in the treatment meted out to the vicar of St Thomas outside Exeter. He was executed as a ringleader and hung from his own tower whilst dressed in his vestments, sacred bell and rosary beads.

One hundred years later, with the execution of King Charles, Devon finished another period of disruption but the Civil War years were merely part of a longer period of defacement and destruction. The church at **Ottery St Mary** was famously attacked by Parliamentary soldiers: they damaged the organ and beheaded effigies. How much of the defacement that can be seen elsewhere today was caused in this period is impossible to know. Some no doubt occurred before and it must be assumed more took place in the following generations. A bench-end at Abbotsham, for example, raises several questions. Why is the face of Jesus intact while those of Mary and John are missing? Closer inspection shows that the head of Jesus was inserted into the woodwork. Was this done originally or was a carver employed later to replace his missing head?

Devon built few churches in the seventeenth century. Plymouth's Charles Church is one of them. Its importance is difficult to gauge since its destruction in the Second World War. It stands as a shell of a church, not dissimilar to how it was for much of the Civil War. Charles Church was begun in 1640 but not finished for another eighteen years.

ABOVE: THE GREAT DOOR AT ST SAVIOUR'S CHURCH, DARTMOUTH
OPPOSITE: ST SAVIOUR'S CHURCH, DARTMOUTH

DEVON'S FIFTY BEST CHURCHES

The long years of reformation also embellished churches. Altar rails began to be introduced in the 1620s and can still be seen at Woodbury and **Plymtree** amongst other places. The rails separated the congregation from the wooden communion tables. These tables had replaced the stone altars (one of which partly survives at Bradford). Murals, which had depicted biblical scenes and saints, were whitewashed and replaced by the Creed and the Lord's Prayer often on wooden boards. Bratton Clovelly is unusual in having an Old Testament scene painted in the seventeenth century. Another interesting one can be seen at Salcombe Regis.

Royal coats of arms were another embellishment. They were introduced to mark the monarch as Head of the Church of England. These, in wood or plaster, can be found throughout Devon for every monarch. One of the most interesting is at Frithelstock which was made of plaster by John Abbot. An earlier one, of 1638, can be seen at Ashwater.

Preachers were being introduced, to supplement clerics, from the late sixteenth century onwards in such places as Exeter, Plymouth and Dartmouth. It was they who found the new pulpits particularly useful. At **Shebbear** is one of Devon's most highly carved pulpits and another is in the chapel of ease at Okehampton but Black Torrington and Braunton are equally pleasing. **Branscombe's** great triple-decker is a joy of the church. Similar pulpits are at Moreleigh and Molland.

New seats were still being introduced such as at **Shebbear** and some are firmly dated like those at Clovelly (1634) and Horwood (1635), all three in North Devon. There are also extraordinary family pews for the Bluetts at **Holcombe Rogus**, the Pine-Coffins at **Alwington** and an individual one for the Earl of Bath at **Tawstock**. Screens continued to be built: there is one of stone at **Colyton** and wooden ones at Rose Ash and Whitestone. Washfield has exuberant wooden carving including a trail of snails and several big-breasted women. The screen also has the coat of arms of James I prominently placed where the rood would formerly have been.

Galleries were built to accommodate the increasing population. These can be seen at such places as Rockbeare, Sandford, **Kentisbeare** and, most interestingly where the woodwork can be compared with surrounding buildings, **Dartmouth St Saviour**.

Shortly after figures in wood and stone had been removed from churches for theological reasons others began to take their place. Great numbers of figurative memorials were erected in the late sixteenth century and this accelerated with the following generations. Whereas statues and images of saints were removed

LADY MARY POLE AT COLYTON

on the grounds that they might be worshipped, their successors, the funerary monuments, were installed on the understanding that these individuals were being commemorated because of their exemplary lives.

Many hundreds of such monuments, of the wealthier element of society, can still be seen today. These were made of slate (such as South Tawton), plaster (Clawton), wood (Christow, **Ashton**, **Parracombe**), brass (Dartmouth St Saviours) but mostly of stone.

A separate style evolved in North Devon which used Somerset alabaster for small medallions which often portrayed the godliness of the deceased. One stunning example, commemorating John Downe, can be seen at Bideford but there are many other examples at **Barnstaple**.

Local floor tiles survive in a number of North Devon churches. These were made from the clay found in and around Fremington from the fourteenth century but many are of the mid-seventeenth to early-eighteenth centuries. A particularly impressive display is at Spreyton, Bradworthy, Parkham and Sutcombe. Few North Devon churches do not have them somewhere underfoot.

The Georgians

The Anglican Church in Devon has often been described as having fallen asleep during the eighteenth century. The clergy were famously derided as being 'on the whole dull and lazy if no worse' and the churches 'were devoid of a living ministry and the parsons addicted to fox hunting'. Devon's greatest historian, W. G. Hoskins, thought Exeter's bishops were 'feeble or slack'. The laxity of the established church in Devon has been challenged, with some success, but it is true that few new churches were built despite a steady growth in the general population. But any resultant rise in congregations which could have led to new building appears to have been offset by the marked rise of the Dissenters in the first half of the eighteenth century. The most notable new churches are St George, built in Tiverton in 1730, and St Aubyn, erected at Devonport in the 1770s to accommodate the spectacular growth in population in the port. Many Anglican churches accommodated greater congregations by inserting galleries and this continued into the early nineteenth century.

Seating evolved with the creation of the horse box pews, sometimes referred to as 'high seats' at the time, which succeeded the earlier benches. Screens continued to be built. That at Cruwys Morchard, erected in the early 1700s, impresses with its grand and classical great Corinthian columns. Pulpits were another continuing embellishment. Perhaps one of the most symbolic innovations was the placing in some churches, including **East Budleigh** and possibly elsewhere, of the pulpit where the rood formerly stood. The congregation had to walk under the pulpit to enter the chancel. Where Jesus was once placed in medieval churches, now stood the cleric giving his sermon. In effect, communicants reached God through his word as delivered by clerics rather than via the saints, angelic host and the sacrifice of Jesus.

26

THE BOX PEWS
AT BIDEFORD

Bideford Church in its
Classic dress!!

Memorials evolved in the Georgian period by using classical motifs, such as urns and figures in ancient dress. Some of the most striking monuments are not in the church but in the churchyards. The best preserved are those made of slate and the most interesting designs can be found in western and northern parts of Devon. Some of the richest graveyards for such stones are Mary and Peter Tavy.

Allied to the slate gravestones are the sundials of North Devon. Those of the Berry family are particularly good, such as that at **Tawstock**. They employed the same materials and skills they used for gravestones and many have similar motifs, such as angels and hour glasses. Brentor is a good example of this.

The painted reredos can be found throughout Devon for this period with good examples still to be seen at Widecombe in the Moor and **South Milton**.

The Victorians and the Oxford Movement

Professor Hoskins felt that the church in Devon continued into the early nineteenth century at a miserable level and credits Henry Philpotts, probably Exeter's most controversial bishop, with starting a revival. In his great history of Devon Hoskins stressed the time most local clerics had spent in hunting, two days a week, rather than tending to their spiritual flocks. He highlighted men like 'the unspeakable oaf' Parson Froude, forty-nine years the vicar of Knowstone, who was said by his successor to be 'guilty of every crime in the calendar'.

What escaped Hoskins' attention was the role of men in the Oxford Movement, those described as Tractarians, who worked for a reinstatement of older traditions to the Anglican church including reforming the buildings. Sowton is one of the earliest of these new churches in Devon but others worth visiting include **St John Torquay** and **Bicton**.

Immediately before the Tractarians' 'arrival' in Devon two local clerics commented in 1828 that in the interior of many Devon churches 'the walls are dirty, the windows broken or partly blocked up, the pavement uneven, the seats, and frequently the pulpit, in a state of decay.' The Oxford movement and the later Cambridge Camden Society were to become controversial and these two clerics argued that in the years before the Victorian period a Protestant was allowed to publicly praise ancestors' Catholic churches 'without any danger of having his faith perverted'.

Stained glass revival was part of this rekindling interest in Gothic architecture and in the general return to the days before the Reformation. Local men, and later women, began to specialise in stained glass, such as Alfred Beer of Exeter, and examples of his and of later Victorians are found in nearly every Devon church. Some early glass was reinserted into windows. This includes Gittisham which has a fascinating array of half-seen images. These include six pigs at a trough, a woman racing to a food-laden table and Christ being taken off the cross and then later laid in his tomb. Hatherleigh, by way of contrast, has Christ on the cross, another roundel is of St Peter and a third, dated 1653, of the Annunciation. Glass is one of the few facets of Victorian church improvement that has received public approval. Historians have been slower to appreciate it for the skill with which it was produced and like the public, or perhaps led by them, have derided the nineteenth century as having ruined churches. It has been forgotten that many buildings were dilapidated and some had urgent work needed. Certainly the scale of change overwhelmed the character of some churches particularly given that in the nineteenth century there was often sufficient money to completely alter the buildings. Whatever the merits of Victorian renovations, refurbishment and rebuilding, it is true to say that the nineteenth century returned colour to many churches. Stained glass is the most noticeable aspect of this.

The Victorians were also fond of the earlier benches and began to take out the box pews. One late Georgian had already advised they were 'greatly superior in accommodation to the ugly square boxes of all sizes and forms with which the greater part of our churches are deformed'. In his opinion it had never been intended that 'a certain class of person should be shut in high partitions to talk or sleep unobserved by the rest of the congregation'. Men such as Harry Hems of Exeter copied the older style and reinserted these benches in churches across Devon. He and others were also employed to reinstate the rood screen and reredos which were often built in ornate and elaborate styles.

There were tensions between the Anglo Catholics and the rest of the Anglican church and this resulted in disputes, particularly during and after the Great War, over what items were appropriate. Shaldon is one of many where this can be seen to have happened.

The Twentieth Century

The last century saw some of the greatest changes to Devon's churches. Bombing during the second world war resulted in the destruction of many in Exeter and Plymouth as well as in smaller communities such as St Marychurch, Aveton Giffard and Clyst St George. The two ancient churches in Plymouth symbolise this loss with one kept as a memorial to the war and the other redefining itself after having been all but destroyed. It now has the most vigorous modern stained glass in Devon.

The building of new churches, which had accelerated under the Victorians, ceased during the war but accelerated in the 1950s and 1960s. More recently there has been an ongoing debate over the removal of historic fabric (increasingly known as reordering) versus the conservation of that heritage. The need is to balance the adapting of buildings to new ways of worship with the preservation of fabric that is unique and precious. Dwindling congregations in some churches has presented yet another problem and one which is likely to accelerate.

The legacy of the last seventeen centuries is we have hundred of churches with many thousands of objects, nearly every one is unique and expresses aspects of Devon's history. Many are unknown and unappreciated beyond their own congregations but deserve to be treasured much more widely. One hundred years ago an admirer of Devon's churches wrote 'Devon may be sleepy, rural, behind the times, but it does set an example to clergy and villages all over the country. Let us hope that there will be no awakening in this country, when churches will be closed and graveyards become the village playground.' A century later there is still the pressing need to appreciate and preserve what is precious and unique in our heritage. In order to do that we need to understand what lies on our very doorsteps.

ST ANDREW'S CHURCH, PLYMOUTH

Using this Guide

Postcode references have been provided for each church as well as a map indication.

At the end of each entry is a note regarding how to access each church: parish officials have agreed whether their church should be designated as open or whether it is by arrangement.

The diocese's website provides telephone numbers for churchwardens and clerics and these are mostly noted at the church itself.

Key

🔑 *Open (green key)*

🔑 *Open by arrangement (orange key)*

🔑 *Closed (red key)*

DEDICATION

For Carole & Ray

1

ALWINGTON

ST ANDREW
POSTCODE: EX39 5DA

There is an intensity and depth to the charm of St Andrew's which lies with the surprising, intriguing and puzzling woodwork.

There are impressive wagon roofs but these escape most visitors because the eye remains at ground level, drawn to the carved wood of all sorts of shapes and sizes. At the east end is an extraordinary reredos with painted panels of Saints Andrew and Peter along the North Devon coast. The paintings cover an earlier Creed and Ten Commandments and were the work of Lady Maude White. The reredos itself is made up in 1806 of carved early-sixteenth century panelling that had been brought from nearby Parkham church. Is the wood from a rood screen? A few years earlier the altar rail had been inserted as was the pulpit, also a conglomeration of reused sixteenth-century bench-ends and roof cornices. The sounding board is imposing and inventive in its construction The carving of the panel behind the vicar is particularly expressive but was there a point to the two faces being seen as he spoke? The carved heraldic arms at the front are those of Richard Coffin who died in 1555.

Some other sixteenth-century bench-ends were retained (along with others from Parkham) to create several panels. The carving is superb and one (in front of the north chapel) is dated 1580. In and around them are also a series of bench-ends from the early twentieth century which were carved by the marvellous Reuben Arnold, a local man. What is not immediately clear is which are ancient and which were carved by Arnold. He also made the lectern, choir stalls and tower screen. It was said that Arnold was inspired by his old illustrated bible.

At the east end of the south aisle is another extraordinary creation, the pew of the Coffin family (they married with the Pine family and have been known since as the Pine-Coffins). Miss Cresswell thought this a 'monstrous structure' but

DETAIL OF WOODWORK

THE FAMILY PEW

this is another wonder of the church, said to have been reassembled from the Pine-Coffins' home where it was the Minstrel Gallery. It is thought to be Jacobean (Miss Creswell wrote it was in the style of) but the woodwork looks surprisingly modern because it has had a dense dark stain applied to it possibly as early as 1819. It is a curious jumble with some later woodwork. The pew has been raised since at least 1848. What is curious is the stone facing beneath the stairs. Does it lead into a family vault full of pine coffins of the Pine-Coffins?

Near to it is a wall monument to Richard and Elizabeth Coffin. The text proclaims that they are one 'joined Coffin' and indeed the monument is unusual in that husband and wife are holding hands. Below them are their fifteen children, with their names (best seen from the family pew) recorded by each of them. This detail is nearly unique in Devon. John, their son and heir, is the male figure in armour. He died shortly after the monument was erected.

The flooring has good ledger stones and North Devon tiles while in the north transept is a fifteenth-century relief of a woman said to be a mermaid but possibly a church benefactor. Before leaving crane your neck for a look at the gargoyles on the tower. In 1848 they were described as 'uncouth animals' but more importantly a century ago they were known as the 'Alwington Bull Dogs' from which the locals took their name. In the tower is also a bell said to ring on its own volition just before the death of the squire.

⚷ *Open by arrangement*

2

ASHTON

ST JOHN THE BAPTIST
POSTCODE: EX6 7QR

The style of the Perpendicular period permeates this building. A sense of isolation and remoteness heightens it. In this church can be enjoyed an unusual survival of a late medieval chapel with glass, painting and woodwork.

Village tradition relates that the south door has two bullet holes from a Civil War skirmish. Inside, the columns are made of Beer stone as is the font which has heraldry indicating it commemorates Sir James Chudleigh's marriage in 1476.

The church is full of Perpendicular benches. In 1793 one commentator thought it 'neat and well seated', in 1828 another approved of the benches for being 'boldly carved, neat and solid' and in 1843 yet another noted modern box pews were built over them.

The main attractions are the rood and parclose screens and in particular their paintings. These are magnificent, particularly those within the chapel and chancel. In 1828 they were modestly complimented as being 'decent not to say spirited'. Careful restoration in 1902 by Exeter's Herbert Read helped their survival. The paintings are among Devon's best.

The west side of the rood screen has 32 saints including a rather camp St George, a full-lipped Mary and a very blond infant Jesus. Many figures are disfigured or mutilated. It is with the large demi-figures inside the rood screen that the church becomes truly remarkable. Here are ten paintings which have their only counterparts in Devon at nearby Bridford. The later ones are on the east side: perhaps they date from the early 1500s? In 1843 James Davidson, Devon's first substantial commentator on churches, speculated these were the work of foreign artists.

The images proclaim the Incarnation, the transformation of God into human flesh through Jesus. The north chapel may have been both a Chudleigh family chapel and a chantry chapel (for saying prayers for the dead). The inscriptions are from the scriptures.

In the mid 1800s the glass was noted as being particularly good. Some later glass is also pleasant. Notice the man's profile within the medallion on the tomb in the East Window. What was its purpose? The main interest lies in the medieval glass fragments of the late 1400s which were probably made by the men who worked at Doddiscombsleigh. The glass was refurbished in 1902 and the restorer, Maurice Drake of Exeter, wrote it was 'an almost matchless example of tireless, patient and diligent labour'. Drake calculated that in order to produce the lioncels, the collection of 24 lions, the glazier had worked for a month merely to prepare them for painting. Drake thought only one visitor in ten thousand could appreciate the 'tender care, the diligence and the loving labour' devoted to the detail of these heraldic shields.

A wooden monument remembers Sir George and Lady Mary Chudleigh. These memorials imitate stone to limit costs but it shows how easily wood can depict family connections. Lady Mary's likeness, as a young woman, can be seen in her father's monument at Plympton St Mary. Sir George was a Parliamentarian but reluctantly supported civil war. The couple had nine sons and nine daughters.

Nearby is a wall-painting which has been interpreted as the mass of St Gregory but see that at Paignton. Alongside Jesus are symbols of his crucifixion including the ladder, scourge, hammer, handkerchief and box, dish, spear, lance, vinegar sponge, pincers and scourge. The mural had been covered by the Chudleighs' memorial until it was moved in about 1900. The monument had been erected in 1657 which indicates the mural was on public view until then. Fragments of paint elsewhere indicate other wall-paintings survive behind plaster and paint.

On the floor near the later drum pulpit is a crude brass memorial to William Honnywell. 'Gntilman' was inserted after his name. At the top is a skull with eyes. Below are the words

THE SCREENS

'in death is life' and a spade and scythe are crossed at the bottom. There are other slab stones of a similar character.

⚷ *Open*

3

ATHERINGTON

ST MARY

POSTCODE: EX37 9HY

$\mathcal{S}$t Mary's Church is like a banquet with one surprising course after another.

The medieval screen is a marvel. Devonians can be complacent about their screens, particularly if unaware of their rarity elsewhere, but that at Atherington is unique even here: it has retained part of its loft.

There are two distinct screens with the main one, that between the chancel and the nave, said to have been taken from Umberleigh chapel. The second screen is four and a half bays long. It is worthwhile deciphering the differences in styles between them while admiring the detail of the carving. The heads are varied and the figures range from fully dressed to nude. Some could be described as playful.

The early sixteenth-century loft is between the nave aisle and chancel aisle and should be viewed from both angles. How it survived the Reformation and the generations that have followed is astonishing. Perhaps the vicars were too busy. Certainly in 1877 the cleric was occupied in countering gossip he was a former policeman turned out of the force for drunkenness. The loft is usefully compared with a partial one at Marwood.

Only at Atherington, with the towering loft, is it possible to contemplate the magnificence of Devon's late medieval churches. This loft has been influential beyond its creators' imaginations. Herbert Read, the Exeter carver, used it as a model because there was no other and replicated it at Kenton and in other churches. But it is at Atherington that the woodwork has an integrity which provokes contemplation.

Wood carving elsewhere is also exciting. The wagon roofs have good bosses and there are angels standing on top of green(ish) men. Sets of poppy head benches line the nave but there are also early choir seats (two with misericordes) and other pews.

There is a mutilated thirteenth-century knight (but of high quality), thought to be Sir William Champernowne of Umberleigh, in the north chancel chapel and three chest tombs in the east chancel arcade. One has two fourteenth-century effigies: these are reputedly Sir Ralph and Lady Eleanor Willington. There is still good detail despite the wear and tear of 700 years. Another has early sixteenth-century brasses to Sir John Bassett and his two wives along with their twelve children. Each family is represented under their own mothers.

A wall monument of 1662 has pleasing Barnstaple alabaster medallions, particularly the winged hourglass and the grinning skull, but more unusual is the slate interior with the holding hands (*see Alwington*) under a flaming heart. The text declares their true love made them one heart. There is what James Davidson described in 1848 as 'brilliant old stained glass' in the north chancel chapel. The medieval Virgin Mary has expressive eyes and the angels could have inspired Shirley Temple's hairdresser.

In the churchyard is the Great War memorial with its sword of sacrifice pointing the wrong way. Its designer, Sir Reginald Blomfield, was Devon-born (at Bow) and deplored the unlicensed uses rural parishes made of his cross. Of this he would have been scathing. Fortunately for Atherington, but unfortunately for him, Blomfield never visited St Mary's.

THE FIFTEEN BASSETS

In the mid 1800s the Exeter Diocesan Architectural Society concluded this was 'a most remarkable church, the screen is most elaborate and has many peculiarities, is unpainted and has canopies and pedestals above them for five figures. At the east end of the chancel aisle is some fine glass with figures of David and his harp, the blessed Virgin and Infant, our Lord with globe and cross and one besides unknown. In the chancel several good monuments, two recumbent figures of the fifteenth century.' 150 years later these are still to be cherished. Atherington has three aspects which perhaps defines a Devon church: it has a west tower, screen and barrel roof and in St Mary's these are exceptional.

⚷— *Open by arrangement*

TOP LEFT: ONE OF THE ROOF ANGELS HOLDING A SHIELD
TOP RIGHT AND MIDDLE RIGHT: DETAILS OF THE SCREEN CARVING
MIDDLE CENTRE: MEDIEVAL GLASS
BOTTOM LEFT: THE SCREEN WITH THE LOFT
BOTTOM RIGHT: A 'POPPY HEAD' BENCHEND

4
BARNSTAPLE

ST PETER
POSTCODE: EX31 1DW

The twisted shape of the leaded spire is one of Barnstaple's familiar features but the main reason for visiting St Peter's lies with how its leading citizens chose to remember themselves four centuries ago. Barnstaple's Elizabethan merchants were prosperous and while many were inclined to Puritanism they nevertheless filled the church with extraordinary monuments which were locally carved. Some memorials were discarded when the church was largely rebuilt in the late 1800s but more than a dozen survive and they express a richness and vitality that epitomised post-Reformation Barnstaple. Seven are figurative and strike melancholy and pious poses. These men and women rest with familiar Resurrection motifs (skulls, bibles and hourglasses) but somehow they also have an air of not just hope but expectant confidence.

Each is different. Richard and Mary Clapham look to one another across a prayer desk while their four sons and five daughters queue below. Her hourglass is half full. Elizabeth Delbridge prays while her infant, who died with her in childbirth, lies below. Yet another woman, twenty-six year old Sarah Shepcott, is wrapped in a shroud with her dead baby. Curtains are pulled back to reveal a smiling Sarah on her side, elbow resting on a skull, while she clutches her dead child. A phoenix rises from the ashes above her. George Peard has one hand upon a skull and the other on the bible but the interesting aspect

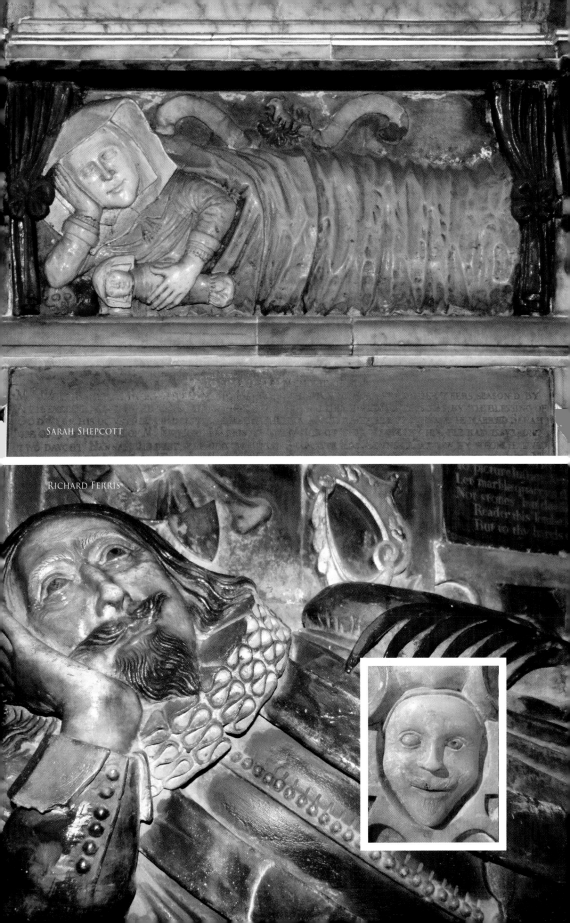

SARAH SHEPCOTT

RICHARD FERRIS

THE CLAPHAMS

DETAIL OF THE CHASUBLE

MARTIN BLAKE

of his monument is he has his left eye open and the right one shut. Peard was a keen supporter of Parliament and was imprisoned by the Royalists shortly before his death. Perhaps he should have had both eyes open. The monument for Richard Ferris, a merchant and mayor during the Civil War who rests on his side near the south door, is unusual in that it has expected death symbols such as a pickaxe, shovel, bones and hourglass on one side but the other side has little-used ones in Devon of a coffin, urn, candles and part of a skull. He looks to heaven and his moustache helps give him a happy countenance; his elbow rests not on a skull or bible but upon a comfortable pillow.

What makes the Barnstaple Workshop different in its monuments is not necessarily the figures but their medallions. Those of Amy Tooker illustrate biblical texts while two for Thomas Horwood depict commerce (ships) and charity (the almshouse he built still stands). The most complex is to nine-year old Nicholas Blake. He has a reflective pose while around him is a flaming heart (indicating his religious fervour). There are four medallions in the immediate framework with Latin text: they read `he restores with grain and flower', ` he glows like the stars; they will be as the angels', `his death is like the flower which springs up and is cut down' and `the days of man are like the span of your hand and man is a bubble'. Five medallions outside the framework refer to his family: William and Mary Blake are depicted with the text `They shall follow the Lamb', his two sisters Elizabeth and Agnes Blake, who pre-deceased him, are shown with `No longer will they hunger or thirst', there are cherubs with God, a congregation with an empty pulpit and finally, Nicholas' father Martin with the text `To die is so much more profit to me than to remain in the flesh'. Martin Blake erected the monument sometime after 1635 and and the empty pulpit refers to his having lost his job as vicar in the 1650s. There is also a note in the memorial that he had yet to be reappointed: in effect, the father used his son's memorial as a means to cite his own religious persecution.

There are other items too interesting to miss. In the north aisle is a seventeenth-century bust of Aaron which was part of the altar screen in 1836. Moses is now missing. Nearby is a Pre-Reformation chasuble which was saved by a churchwarden and returned in 1910 by his family.

⚷ *Open*

5
BERE FERRERS

ST ANDREW
POSTCODE: PL20 7J

St Andrew's situation charms the visitor and provides the dead with a view of the river Tavy as it meets the Tamar. This is also the only church for which a man died to record stained glass.

St Andrew's is a good example of a richly endowed Arch presbytery where five priests celebrated mass at five altars. It has outstanding fourteenth-century monuments, glass and tracery as well as its overall plan.

The font is surprising: this late Norman tub has a low decorated girdle. A walk down the nave is through a forest of oak benches of the early 1500s. Their ends are delicately carved and there are heraldic shields, notably for the Ferrers family with their horseshoes. By 1848 box pews had been built on the benches. The remnant of the earlier rood screen has faint ghosts of the original figures.

Pale stone of the fourteenth to sixteenth centuries runs throughout but in the morning the eye is drawn to the East Window. It was here that in 1821 Charles Stothard, an artist known for depicting ancient monuments, was standing on a gardener's ladder when a rung broke. He fell to his death. A tile marks the spot. The inscription on his memorial (on the exterior) has nearly worn away. Next to it has been repositioned (with a ghoulish sense of humour?) a slate to Walter Pyke who met a similar fate.

> *By a fall I caught my death*
> *Which no man knows his time or breath*
> *I might have dyed as soon as then*
> *Had I been with Physician men.*

LEFT: The knight at prayer
ABOVE: The sun and the moon   BELOW: The Norman font

The East Window is striking. Six panels of fourteenth-century glass are set. The top depicts, from the left, a knight with a church, a devotional woman, Christ, a woman instructing a boy to read, a knight praying and at the base a male figure, possibly a pilgrim. Notice two figures with a sun and a moon in the lowest panel. The glass was clearly commissioned by the Ferrers family. The text about them has been largely lost although in one instance can be read *Ne Wills Fereys me fecit* (William Ferrers made this). The glass has a chequered history which impedes interpretation. It was stored in a box shortly after Stothard died, reinserted in 1871, taken out during the second world war and then returned in 1946. The re-assemblages are confusing. Segments of the boy's clothing appear to have been used in other panels and other pieces of glass look as though they were inaccurately placed. Nine roundels of ancient glass are at the apex of the window. Are these all the dead at the Resurrection?

On the north wall of the chancel lies a highly carved monument. It was on this stone that Stothard died. These are two stone effigies of the early 1300s which are related

ABOVE: THE TWO KNIGHTS
OPPOSITE: INSTRUCTING A BOY IN READING

to work at Exeter Cathedral and are amongst the finest in Devon. A knight and his lady rest under an ornate arched canopy but it is debatable whether these are William de Ferrers and his wife Isolde or their son William and daughter-in-law Matilda.

A second knight, of a similar date and quality, is in the north transept. He, most likely another Ferrers, has chain mail, crossed his legs and still grips his sword. After some 700 years it still possible to make out his eyes, brows and teeth. This transept has in its centre a tomb chest of Purbeck stone (possibly of the 1520s with panelled sides depicting shields), an elegantly carved slab (which may have formed the ceiling of a tomb) and an early carved stone with a cross (which may have been a memorial stone).

Dog-owners will approve of the theory that a cat in the ribbed ceiling of the porch represents 'evils and dangers'. This is plausible but unfortunately the carving is more likely to be a demon.

There are gravestones to cholera victims and on the south west corner of the church is a monument to one John Pearse with musical notes from the hymn *'I know that my Redeemer lives'*. The use of the notes is almost unique in Devon.

⚷ *Open*

48

BICTON

ST MARY AND THE MAUSOLEUM
POSTCODE: EX9 7BL

T he *'Gem of the West'*, as it was called at the time, was consecrated in March 1850. Louisa Lady Rolle, the patron of the church, provided the funds, as she would later for the new church at Otterton. St Mary's was on her doorstep; there was no village of Bicton but only her large estate which was centred at the mansion house not far from her new church. The grounds remain among the most impressive in Devon and provide an extraordinary setting for the church. Near it were once set the parish stocks and as late as 1879 there was a sign placed on them *'Boys Beware'*. Women were also warned *'Take off your pattens'* which was not meant for the churchyard but for the fine floors of the church. Given these were the grounds of an aristocratic family, it is not surprising that Bicton often hosted royal parties and key national figures. One such personage was Winston Churchill who in 1927 warned a huge crowd of the dangers of Bolsheviks and trade unions. He also asked of the Great War *'what was it all for?'*.

This gem was designed by John Hayward, an Exeter architect who erected other similar buildings, and it conformed to the principles of the Camden Society and the Gothic Revival. The church is a testament to the Ecclesiological movement as a conscious effort to return to a perceived church of medieval England. It is in cruciform form and retains much of its original interior. There are specially commissioned Minton tiles which feature the Rolle Arms and Lady Louisa's monogram. Two windows of stained glass by the London firm of Warrington have relatively recently been removed but the others remain. The lectern is also later but the ornate font was installed in 1850 as were the oak pews and the altar. The carvings around the Caen-stone font are beautifully detailed although some are

DENNIS ROLLE'S MONUMENT

STAINED GLASS IN THE MAUSOLEUM

slightly bruised by daily wear and tear. Also inside are eighteen theologians, carved in stone, looking down from on high. Running around the exterior of the church are carvings of forty-eight of England's monarchs and, surprisingly, Oliver Cromwell. Lord and Lady Rolle are by the north door through which she would have entered from Bicton House. St Mary's can usefully be compared not merely with Otterton but with Sowton and Torquay's St John along with that range of other Victorian churches in the English Riviera.

Lady Rolle intended the church as a monument to her late husband and his own church was demolished to make way for it. It was said to be ruinous, although just a few years beforehand the Exeter Diocesan Architectural Society failed to notice this when a representative visited. Two generations earlier the beauty of the situation was noted by Reverend Swete in 1795 when he wrote 'scenery more picturesque than this cannot well be conceived'.

In the autumn of 1849 Augustus Welby Northmore Pugin was employed to direct the creation of a mausoleum (or mortuary chapel as he termed it) out of the old church. He chose to use the south chantry and the work was finished in 1852, the year in which he suddenly died at the age of 40. In effect, he destroyed one medieval building in order to recreate a new one. At the start of his career Pugin stated that stylistically he sought to revive and not invent. This he did at Bicton not only with the design but with the building itself. Pugin did little to change the structure of the existing chapel: he retained the two existing windows and three exterior walls. A fourth wall was built on the north side which had led from the chancel into the chapel and he created a new door in the south side. Pugin also retained the tower which stands independently at the west end. The south wall of the nave serves to connect the mausoleum with the tower.

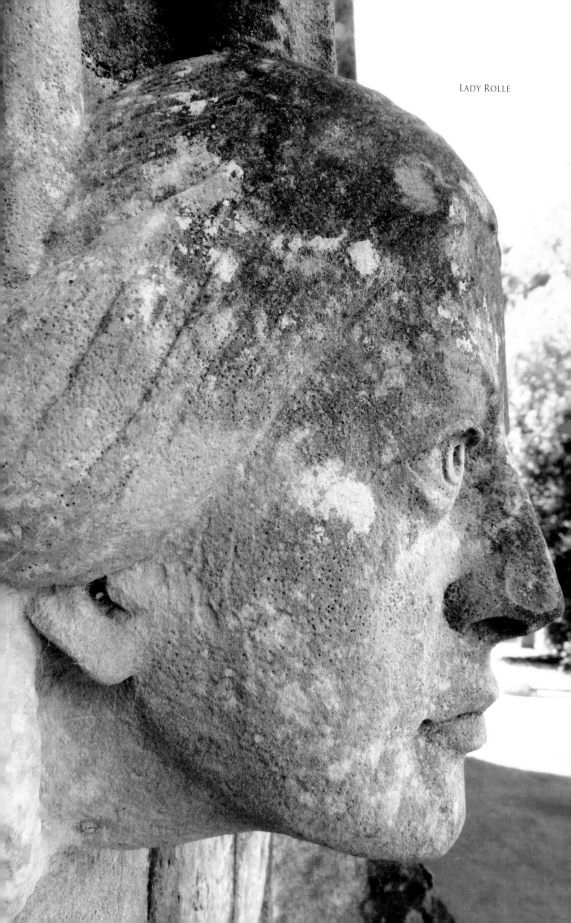

LADY ROLLE

The interior is Pugin's main creation: delicate carving, strong vivid painting in the vaulted ceiling, two large glass windows by Hardman, vigorous stone carving and striking Minton tiles. The effect is stunning and should be judged with Hayward's own creation of the same date a few feet to the east. The contrast between the exterior and interior is marked: the ruins are atmospheric, sombre and melancholy but inside there is a grandeur which is both solemn and surprisingly uplifting.

The Mausoleum has two monuments. One is for a Rolle ancestor of the 1630s which was kept in its existing position along the south wall. The quality of the carving is superb and looks untouched after nearly 400 years. Dennis and Margaret Rolle lie on their death beds with their baby placed beneath them nearly on the floor. One observer, more than 300 years ago, noted that Dennis Rolle was born on the shortest day of the year and died on the longest. He was also, according to Reverend Prince in about 1700, 'the darling of his country'. The monument, Prince noted, was 'lively and curiously cut'. This is still true three centuries later. Their baby's head rests with a skull placed underneath his cushion. Across from them is John Lord Rolle, some 200 years later. The tomb chest was designed by Pugin and carved by George Myers' workshop in London.

The Mausoleum is a significant work and hard to reconcile as the gift of a widow who was so angry on discovering the terms of her husband's will that she burned his favourite things on Bicton's lawn in a great bonfire.

What would she, a 46 year old woman with a husband twice her age at 92, have erected had she been happier with him or had she already forgiven him in death?

🗝 *St Mary's Open via Bicton Park Botanical*
🗝 *Gardens. The Mausoleum is private.*

PUGIN'S CEILING

8

BRANSCOMBE

ST WINIFRED
POSTCODE: EX19 3AX

There is a cheerfulness to this well-kept church, particularly on a bright sunny day. In the mid 1800s it was noted as 'a most interesting church, substantial and in neat order' but fifty or so years later, in 1910, it was described as being in a deplorable state. Miss Cresswell wrote 'damp, dilapidation, neglect all combined in a scene of dirt and desolation, kept locked and exhibited by a apologetic sexton who observed there was nothing to see'. The wet had produced green and brown stains which gave the appearance of frescoes. Fortunately a restoration programme occurred shortly afterwards which has resulted in the survival of what is a fascinating building.

The position of the church, set back from the sea in a wooded valley, is appealing in itself and it allows the visitor to appreciate that the tower is centrally placed. In 1801 one imaginative visitor commented 'the tinkling bell of which, when its sound floats through the vale, suggests the idea of some lone convent, that at stated periods calls the scattered inhabitants of an Alpine village to their unostentatious devotions'. Along the south east exterior wall of the church are a series of Roman numerals cut into the stonework. These, still sharp, have been interpreted as a sun dial.

The exposed local white stone provides evidence of the Normans and possibly Saxons at the base of the tower. Much of the tower is from the twelfth century and there was building through to the fifteenth century when the church was refurbished. The stone lends itself to carving including, in one place internally, the head of a devil. Despite the small size of the church there seems a surfeit of items of good interest. The three-tier pulpit, in which the vicar spoke from the top, is an

TOP LEFT: DETAIL OF THE FONT
CENTRE LEFT: A DEMON
ABOVE RIGHT: THE PULPIT
BELOW: THE WALL PAINTING

BRANSCOMBE CHURCH CIRCA 1900

unusual survival for Devon. The height must have made him an imposing figure. Along the north wall are the remains of a wall painting which has been thought to represent the sin of lust.

Other colour remnants can be found throughout the church. The font was carved of Beer stone in the fifteenth century but it has been in the church only since 1911 when it was brought from Teignmouth. Notice the foliage erupting from the mouth of a green(ish) man. One hundred years ago Miss Cresswell approved of retaining some box pews 'as specimens of what not to use'. The communion rails are early (seventeenth century) and of the same date or earlier is the gallery. There is also a carved panel which might be Flemish: the Nativity and the Garden of Eden are depicted.

Two early slab memorials with crosses can be found and there are also two exceptional monuments to Cornish women who moved to Branscombe. One lies in the north transept and commemorates Joan Wadham who died in 1583. Perhaps, as in life, she put her husbands first: they face one another at prayer while she is depicted behind them with their children. It was said that she had twenty children one of whom was Nicholas who founded Wadham College. The monument's style is similar to that of the well-known memorial to Mathew Godwin in Exeter Cathedral. In the south transept is another to Anne Bartlett. It was erected less than a generation later in 1607 and was carved from Beer stone. This pale colour runs through the church and is in stark contrast to the character of others in the rest of Devon. In the churchyard are some eighteenth-century carved monuments, with depictions of skulls and angels, which demonstrate how slate stones wear away less easily. An Edwardian visitor noted one of 1658 to a father and son with the surname Lees:

> The wine that in these earthen vessels lay,
> The hand of death hath lately drawn away,
> And as a present served it up on high,
> Whilst here the vessels with the Lees do lie.

🔑 *Open*

9

BRENTOR

ST MICHAEL
POSTCODE: PL19 0NP

*L*ong before the path to the church is taken there are glimpses of it from miles around. Brentor is an experience, an uncommon church in an unlikely place. St Michael's is positioned on an extinct volcano and around it lie the remains of a prehistoric and possibly post-Roman settlement. Few can reach the porch and rest without a struggle. Two hundred years ago one commentator noted that the vicar was forced in bad weather to climb to the church on all fours but his toils must have been light compared to the men who took bodies for burial and for those who carried their stone monuments. Two hundred years ago one visiting vicar pondered why a previous generation would have chosen such a difficult position. He questioned whether 'their thoughts would savour less of the earth or that their prayers would wing a quicker flight to heaven?' The cleric concluded that there should have been some thought given to the extra expense of such a locality let alone the inconvenience. Irrespective, the views are so satisfying at each step up the hill, to Dartmoor, Bodmin and far beyond, that there is no embarrassment in having continual pauses to appraise them.

The church was restored in the 1800s but is mainly of the thirteenth and fifteenth centuries. Even so, the bareness of the interior will defeat most visitors from understanding its construction and few last more than a few moments before filing back out to enjoy the views. The church comprises a nave and sanctuary. This is why a century ago local women told their children 'if you get into the second aisle of Brent Tor church you will never get out'. The tower and font are fifteenth century, the nave and north window are thirteenth century while the south window may be from the twelfth century. This becomes all the more

THE NAVE

extraordinary when one considers that local people climbed each Sunday morning to worship here for nearly 900 years. For a small portion of that time, a hundred years or so, visitors have been scrawling their names inside the porch roof. This is the only church in Devon that has this practice and is mostly due to there being little else to do at the top.

One aspect escapes visitors: a memorial stone on the north side and the sundial on the south side are curiously related. The same angel sits at each apex. The sundial has the date 1694 and the initials WR above a sun with incomplete rays. At the base is carved WALTER BATTEN and at the edges are the initials WB interspersed with an abstract design. The memorial on the north side is similar. It has the same initials and a similar abstract symbol but beneath the angel is a series of identical profiles of a man or woman linked together by a circle. Near the base and within an enlarged version of this profile was cut the figure of a woman. The text for the memorial, which has been on the exterior of the church since at least 1848, reads:

> 'Heare under this stone lyeth the body of Walter Batten of brimsabach who was buried april the six in 1677 allso Alce his wife was buried the third of desember 1681'

In Latin was cut the phrase 'remember you will die'. The two stones are some of the most oddly cut in Devon and in such an unlikely place.

A century ago the Reverend Baring Gould told the story of Margery Palmer, an ancient bald, blind, deaf and one-toothed dwarf who lived in the tower and climbed down the bell ropes to accost visitors. On dark winters days in Brentor Church this is one of his more plausible tales.

 Open

10

COLYTON

ST ANDREW
POSTCODE: EX24 6LJ

olyton is curiously satisfying, there is an underlying smartness to the trim houses made carefully with local flint. The church has an octagonal tower which is centrally placed and again, it has an air of satisfaction. Even the cock weathervane seems content.

This church has an easy ability to inspire: the light through the West Window on a summer's day is magnificent, the two Georgian candelabras are wonderfully over the top and the interior feels lofty and cheerful.

This is despite a destructive fire in 1933 which destroyed the roofs of the nave and south aisle. Much of the remaining fabric was saved and the fire revealed parts of a Saxon cross of the tenth century, a rarity in Devon. It stands in a corner. The stone screen is stately. It was built on the eve of the Reformation and crosses the south chancel chapel. This is a remarkable copy of the Lady Chapel screen at Exeter Cathedral. A Jacobean one lies before that of the north chapel.

It is impossible to ignore the post-Reformation monuments: they were built to be noticed and dominate parts of the church in particular the Pole Chapel. There is a wooden tablet to Grace Pole. Another, made from Beer stone, is to William Westofer, also of the early 1600s, and depicts him with his wife and daughter at prayer. These are striking memorials but each varies considerably. That to Mary Pole appears to have been made by two different masons: one material is for the top and another for the base. It remembers not just her but her nine living children. Interestingly, the inscription notes she had two other sons who predeceased her and that these eleven children were born during a marriage of twenty-two years and ten months. She died, most likely of exhaustion, at the age of 38.

SIR JOHN POLE

Two other monuments stand to the memory of William and Katherine Pole who died in 1587 and 1588. It is likely that their son erected both monuments but they have been squeezed into the chapel like two overly-expensive cars into a small garage. The children around Katherine, seven of them, and she herself were crudely executed.

The most striking Pole monument straddles the chapel. Sir John Pole died in 1658 and his body was brought from Kent three months later. He, and his wife Elizabeth, who died thirty years earlier, lean back-to-back on their elbows to face any visitor. A century ago Beatrix Cresswell commented they were `as if tired in this life of looking at each other'. The monument towers over the chapel and barely fits in. The figures are not terribly accomplished (one Edwardian regarded them as 'clumsily realistic') but Sir John has tremendous hair for a man of seventy years. Notice the two infants at the couple's feet.

Margaret Beaufort Countess of Devon has an unsettling presence. Her monument was erected in the early 1400s but restored in the 1800s in part by Harry Hems of Exeter. He was under the impression it was that to a child and modelled the countess' replacement head on that of his granddaughter. Notice most of the other heads have also been replaced but take in the overall grandeur. Cresswell, who could be a sharp critic, noted that Hems compensated for the small head of the Countess by enlarging that of the Virgin Mary. For some time this was wrongly thought to be an effigy of a Courtenay who died choking on a fish bone, hence the effigy's nickname was 'little choke-a-bone'.

The Yonges were Colyton's other longstanding gentry family. Although they had the North Chapel as a mortuary there are no memorials equal to the Poles. One Victorian writer related how it was used as the vestry in the late 1800s when a 'portly-sized' churchwarden, in full flow during a well-attended meeting, suddenly disappeared 'amidst dust and clatter' into the family vault below. The writer used the opportunity to salvage Georgian brasses from the mouldering coffins and placed them on the chapel's walls.

⌐ *Open*

11

CREDITON

HOLY CROSS
POSTCODE: EX17 2AH

The nature of the Church of the Holy Cross can be elusive to the first time visitor but it gradual unravels. From the outside can one appreciate its grandness, comparable in Devon only to Ottery St Mary and Exeter Cathedral. It is reminiscent of them in its dimensions but the facing in local red stone makes it instantly recognisable, an echo of the soil in and around Crediton as well as of the Red Ruby cattle grazing in the local fields.

Most Devonians are aware that Crediton had Devon's Saxon Cathedral but no vestiges of it have survived. Even its Norman replacement is invisible from the outside. What one sees from the High Street is largely a fifteenth-century rebuild which escaped the Great Fire of 1743 unlike most of Crediton.

The view from the south porch is surprising. The height is accented by the clerestory, with light pouring through. The perspective is restricted by the central tower where the lower stonework is Norman with snakes a noticeable decorative feature. The nave served as the parish church and in it is the startling memorial to one of Crediton's principal sons, General Sir Redvers Buller, of whom many Kirtonians still feel immensely proud although his reputation remains under a cloud elsewhere. It states his countrymen erected it. Less obvious are the nature of the figures. The designer, W. D. Caröe, a leading figure in the Arts & Crafts movement, placed God at the top and surrounded him with angels but below, to reflect Buller's military career, there are four religious warriors (St Michael, Joshua, a Crusader and St George). The memorial dominates the nave with vigour.

The nave's pews were carved of English oak for Victoria's Jubilee in 1887. The vicar was the first to demolish the Georgian box pews: with a crowbar and

hammer in hand he said 'it has been the dream of my life to see the old pews swept away'. Much of the interior was renovated in the mid to late 1800s but two impressive earlier monuments were retained: those to Sir William Peryam and Elizabeth Tuckfield are in the chancel. Both deserve attention: she looks to heaven and misses her extremities as well as her face. In 1793 Reverend Polwhele, an early Devon antiquarian, thought the monument was 'most miserably executed' and noted her arms were 'obliterated'. Peryam has fared better: the lines on his

ELIZABETH TUCKFIELD'S MONUMENT

forehead are greater than those elsewhere on his face made by later defilers. He has been remembered for his religious zeal, integrity and learning. These may have contributed to the furrows on his brow or it may have been his three marriages.

Opposite the monuments are fifteenth-century sedilia, the stone seats used for officiating priests, with rich and delicate carving. The graffiti includes two early figures. Is one Elizabethan? On the opposite side is a richly carved tomb recess of the same date, with similar colouring and defaced angels. Behind the Victorian reredos lies the fifteenth-century wall which separates the chancel from what is now the Lady Chapel. From the early 1100s until 1545 it housed a college with between 12 and 18 clerics and then the grammar school for the next three centuries.

Upstairs, entered via a door in the south choir aisle, is the Chapter House on three floors. On the first floor is the Governors' Room, now a museum. Amongst the treasures are two angel bosses. The nave's roof was reconstructed in about 1798 and it was recorded later that the governors used the discarded carved timbers to warm the Chapter House and the Governors' Room. It was remembered that a governor would say to the sexton, 'Put on another angel, William'.

Also not to be missed: the fourteenth-century stone effigies of Sir John de Sully and his wife, the early sixteenth-century French chest in the north chapel with superb carving and the organ, a Great War memorial to, amongst others, Harold Charles Organ, the organist.

⚷ *Open*

OPPOSITE: ONE OF THE ANGELS NOT FOUND BY WILLIAM

12

CULLOMPTON

ST ANDREW
POSTCODE: EX15 1JU

There is a splendour and magnificence to St Andrew's which is completely at odds with the town. No building in Cullompton is its equal nor is it likely there ever will be one. Two hundred years ago it was, in the view of Devon's leading writer of the Picturesque, 'the only edifice commanding a moment's attention'.

The tower is impressive in its own right. It fills the skyline and on close inspection there can be seen three panels, that of the Crucifixion is most easily distinguished. Surprisingly this is Reformation-era decoration, carved in the 1540s.

Like Tiverton, Cullompton's prize attraction is a chapel built in the early 1500s by a cloth merchant. Both are on the south side, have exterior depictions of merchant ships and scenes from Christ's life. The similarities are striking.

The nave is impressive but the Lane Aisle is by itself breathtaking. The fan vaulting is graceful and elegant, the light coming through the window fills the space with an airiness matched by the flow of the lines. It was no mistake that the architect chose angels to peer down from heaven. Along the columns are saints carved into niches. The Dorset Aisle in **Ottery St Mary** is comparable but here the light from the south windows transforms the space. John Lane was a cloth merchant and his trade emblems can be seen in his aisle: besides the ships on the exterior, angels in the aisles hold cloth shears, teasel frames and Lane's own merchant's mark. Along the exterior of the aisle is a message imploring the reader to pray for the souls of Lane and his wife. Nearly 300 years later a visitor noted the text:

THE LANE AISLE

`In honour of God and his blessed mother Mary, remember the souls of John Lane, **Wapentaki Custos, Lanarius** [keeper of the wool] and the soul of Thomasine his wife, to have in memory, with all other their children and friends of your own charity; which were founders of this chapel, and here lie in sepulchre, the year of our lord, one thousand five hundred and six and twenty. God of his grace on both their souls to have mercy and finally bring them to the eternal glory, Amen, for charity.'

Lane's reasons for building the chapel are clear.

Here in the chapel is Cullompton's other famous attraction, its Golgotha. During the Reformation these two pieces of oak were removed from the rood screen and by the early 1900s were being stored in the tower. This is an extremely rare survival for England that has been regarded as one of the most significant examples of fifteenth-century art in the country. The skulls and bones were meant to depict the site of the crucifixion, Golgotha, the place of the skull. Traces of green paint can be seen.

DETAIL: THE GOLGOTHA

ONE OF THE MANY CARVINGS

Even without the Lane Aisle and the Golgotha, St Andrew's would be worth a visit. There are a multitude of interesting stone carvings on the pillars: these corbels are inventive and some almost playful. The early fifteenth-century screen, termed 'a splendid specimen of art' by one commentator in 1843, comprises eleven bays and another two are in the tower. It was repainted in 1849 but was 'disfigured by a hideous coat of paint' in the subsequent opinion of Lady Rosalind Northcote. The south parclose screen may be older still and the north is later but has well-carved angels linking heraldry at the top. The elegant pulpit is early but is it really of the fourteenth century? The font is Norman and the West Gallery is Jacobean. It has a pair of shears at one end and carved figures across its length. Two war memorials are worth investigating. That to the Great War (in the Lane Aisle) is the only one in Devon to depict a man leaving his wife and child for war and then entering heaven. The Second World War memorial is a glass window with good figures of the services. The church demands more time than most visitors would reasonably anticipate.

⚷ *Open*

13

DARTMOUTH

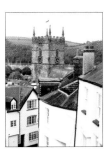

ST SAVIOUR
POSTCODE: TQ6 9DL

Τhis church is a testament to the growing mercantile prosperity of medieval Dartmouth. St Saviour's was dedicated in 1372 but building had begun earlier. It was positioned within the town partly because the existing parish church was up the steep hill to the north but it was also where the town was expanding onto the mud flats which ran between the two hills. This was a Dartmouth Corporation entity (it had the advowson for 250 years from 1585) and the councillors' hands are all over the fabric.

At the south entrance is the staggering wooden door with two Plantagenet lions or leopards across a tree with exaggerated leaves. The date, 1631, records its refurbishment rather than its medieval erection. The visitor arrives under the West Gallery, built as part of a four-year refurbishment of the mid 1630s. The painting features men of the council and the carving is reminiscent of that found in nearby merchant houses. There is no evidence for the speculation that a Spanish vessel captured in the Armada provided the wood. The West Gallery was one of three galleries: in the early 1800s two others ran along the north and south sides. Note that the existing supporting timber arch was inserted in the nineteenth century. Almost underneath the gallery is the plain font which is marginally more interesting by it being fourteenth-century.

There are four items of great interest in the east end. The pulpit, which once stood at the centre of the screen, was described by the expert, Bligh Bond, as 'florid fifteenth-century work'. This highly-painted and elaborately-decorated creation was embellished with the wooden royal badges of King Charles II for his visit

in 1671. These were inserted in the spaces previously occupied by what must have been Catholic statues. The rood screen is mentioned in the church accounts in 1496. This was carved of oak and comprises eleven bays. The south end was partly replaced in 1598. Some figurative painting has survived, although defaced, and there is much colour some of it ancient.

Inside the chancel can be seen the Elizabethan parclose screens. It is also here that one of the great features of St Saviour's lies. In the centre of the floor is an early fifteenth-century brass in memory of John Hawley and his two wives. The lions have faces as surprised as those on the south door. Because of Hawley Devon has a second Hoe, a companion to that at Plymouth. The ancient Dartmouth saying is:

> *Blow the wind high, blow the wind low,*
> *It bloweth good to Hawley's Hoe.*

DETAIL OF THE PULPIT

Hawley's mercantile enterprises were responsible for the rhyme and the place name has been corrupted to Hawley's Haw or Hawley's Hall. Hawley, long wished for as Chaucer's inspiration for the Shipman, ranks as one of Dartmouth's principal sons.

On the north wall of the chancel is another remarkable monument: that to Nicholas Hayman and it features Death as a grinning skeleton, not Father Time, wrapped in a shroud while wielding a scythe in his right hand and an hour glass in his left.

In the chancel is also the extraordinary altar table of 1893 which was made from the existing one of 1588. The Victorians kept the four table legs to use as frontal decoration. These four figures, with their great bulbous noses, are meant to be the four evangelists and, as unlikely as it sounds, was described as handsome carvings in 1847. The writer, James Davidson, also thought they were very ancient and curious. Nevertheless, the angel at St Mathew's shoulder looks almost demonic. The painting was done by George William Ostrehan.

It is worth having a view from the West Gallery. Before the stairs is the largest painting in a Devon church (`The Widow's Son' by William Brockedon).

🗝 *Open (chancel open by arrangement).*

TOP LEFT: THE PULPIT
TOP RIGHT: THE FAMOUS DOOR
BELOW LEFT: THE BRASS OF JOHN HAWLEY
BELOW RIGHT: ST MATHEW AND HIS ANGEL

14

DODDISCOMBSLEIGH

ST MICHAEL
POSTCODE: EX6 7PT

here is a wealth of vivid but concentrated colour inside which no visitor can anticipate. The medieval glass is the most remarkable in Devon outside of Exeter Cathedral and was remarked upon as early as 1793. By the mid 1800s a local hostelry advised visitors the church had 'terrible fine picture windows'. Local tourists have seldom had such good advice. What is striking about this is that James Davidson, Devon's great early commentator on churches, did not notice the great north windows. He visited in 1843 and, although he regarded St Michael's as 'an ancient and venerable structure and well worthy of investigation', his description falls short of the detail he was otherwise capable of.

The east window in the north aisle depicts the seven sacraments and was created by a workshop probably at Exeter in about 1480. These depict:

Eucharist		Ordination
Marriage	**CHRIST**	Baptism
Confirmation		Extreme Unction
	Penitence	

It is easy to see how the glass could have been used as teaching aids and it is possible to imagine that it was told that one female figure, who appears as the left figure on the three bottom panels and in two of the others, had it explained as her life story: from her marriage through to the baptism of her child, his confirmation (and ordination?) and finally a family death. But then again, each woman has the

CONFIRMATION

same face and one way was used to do noses and eyes. Only their hair and clothing distinguish them from one another.

Repairs are known on at least two occasions. The earlier instance can be seen in the extreme unction panel: a blue pane of glass has the words 'Peter Cole glazier done this window March 1762 whom god preserve amen'. Another similar note is in the penance window. Less than 100 years later the Exeter Diocesan Architectural Society recorded 'the best glass in the county is found in the east window of the north chancel... dilapidation is great in the chancel and the remains of the fine glass is allowed to fall out without the least heed being taken

DETAIL OF ST JOHN

to preserve it'. However, within a generation, in 1877, there was a restoration: the central figure of Christ was supplied by Clayton and Bell, a London firm, and they also are responsible for the head of the ginger-haired figure in blue in the baptismal panel. Notice how different his face is from all those around him and that the glass has aged, and attracted grime, in a different manner. This is also apparent from the exterior side of the glass. It is easy to overlook the red lines leading from Christ's wounds (from which his blood travels to the sacraments), the rather modern-looking chair and the slip-on shoes.

There are also four medieval windows on the north side and some have Victorian replacement faces. The figures are Window One St Christopher (new face for the child), St Michael (new demons), St Peter; Window Two St John (new face), the Virgin Mary and St Paul; Window Three St Patrick (new face), St George, St Andrew; Window Four Edward the Confessor and St James the Greater (new face) with the Holy Trinity between them. The initials of the restorer, Clayton & Bell, can be seen in the red clothing of the Virgin Mary along with the date 1879. In 1830 the cleric summarised this glass as depicting St George, St Andrew, St Peter, St Helena with a cross and another St Peter (but with an oar).

It is curious that the glass survived not merely the Reformation but also attacks during the Civil War. One of the early bench-ends appears to have been defaced (a man's nose is missing) but there is no indication the glass was targeted The later glass is not without interest. The east window is by Drake of Exeter as may be two south windows. One is a good first world war memorial. It is worth noticing the early medieval font, an eighteenth-century drum pulpit and the sixteenth-century bench-ends but these seem dull and uninteresting after the glory of the glass.

⚷— *Open*

OPPOSITE: BAPTISM

15
EAST BUDLEIGH

ALL SAINTS
POSTCODE: EX9 7DU

for some time the name this church was most associated with was Noddy. He was said to have attempted to fly from the tower with artificial wings but fell to his death. Village tradition for some 400 years was a gravestone stood in the churchyard. On it was written *'Pray for the soul of Radulphi Node'*. More recently, particularly since the Victorians, the name of Raleigh is more commonly associated with the village and not surprisingly the church has reminders throughout of what is one of Devon's most famous families. In one corner there is even a copy of Zuccaro's portrait of Sir Walter. At the head of the nave is a Raleigh stone slab of the late 1500s. It is in memory of Joan, widow of Otto Gilbert and first wife of Walter, the father of Sir Walter. It is inscribed with a fleuree cross on a pedestal framed by an inscription done in mirror writing. It reads:

'ORATE PRO AIA JOHANNE RALEYH OXTS WALTRI RAILE ARMIG QUE OBIIT X DIE MENSI JUNII ANO D...'.

Sir Walter must have been fairly familiar with the church in those years before he left Devon, before he was known for tobacco, his cloak or Virginia, to make his way in the world. Presumably it was he who arranged for this monument.

All Saints is largely an early fifteenth-century church which was restored in 1884. There is a fifteenth-century font and it along with the columns are made of stone from nearby Beer. In many churches the screen would be an object of interest. It has some later repair work (and the tower screen is a later copy) but as fine as the tracery is it is rare that many visitors spend much time inspecting it. In the chancel itself is a striking painting of the Virgin and Child. This was the work

One of East Budleigh's extraordinary benchends

A SERIES OF BENCHENDS

of Edward Aveling Green, a pupil of Burne Jones. His work is easily overlooked because of the wealth of objects elsewhere.

Instead the eye is drawn to some five dozen late medieval benches. Interestingly these are all secular; not one has a religious symbol. The benches are thought to have been carved in the early 1500s and although similar in style each is individual. They have wreathed foliage framing a unique design. One in particular has attracted attention. In the north aisle, near the chancel, can be found the profile of a man. He has been described as a Native American but this is unlikely not merely because he is bearded. Devonians were not in the Americas until at least the 1540s and no such Americans are known to have been in Devon until the 1580s. Similar floral grotesques can be found in other local churches.

Some benches indicate family sponsors. One bears the Raleigh arms and the date 1537. Presumably this was the family pew. The arms of the St Clere family appear on another and above it was carved a man with a great moustache. Another appears to be that of a wool merchant; it features cloth shears, comb, a bowl of teasels and Bishop Blaize, the patron saint of cloth-makers.

One of the most intriguing is that of a woman facing a dressed chicken. Below a half-door her left hand holds a platter and her right clutches the tail of what has been interpreted as a turnspit dog. A visitor in about 1872 somehow thought it was a sheep. On another bench can be seen a figure, possibly a man, wearing a close-fitting cap and consuming what could be a chicken drumstick.

There is also a particularly detailed ship with two sailors in the rigging, a dory at anchor and an embattled building in the background. Another has a dog chasing his tail. Perhaps one of the most intriguing is the distorted figure below a coat of arms: is this meant to be an African child? Not to be overlooked are a number of Great War benches which have good and unusual representations of the war.

⚷ *Open*

16

EGGESFORD

ALL SAINTS
POSTCODE: EX18 7QU

The Norman font is interesting and the stained glass vaguely appealing but there are three other distinct reasons for visiting this church. This is a building dominated by a need to be remembered and to do so ostentatiously.

The church sits gently above the Taw river in a isolated position. In fact it feels as though it was placed temporarilly. The building is a mixture of the fifteenth century with a renovation in 1867. It was in that year that one of the main attractions of this church, a memorial, was moved from the north room of the chancel to be placed in its current location. The monuments dominate the church and are, according to Miss Cresswell a century ago, more suited to a cathedral than to a small village church. It is the small size of this building and the general lack of other ornamentation that makes these memorials all the more noticeable.

Straight ahead from the north door is the first great monument. It takes the place of a south door. Here Arthur, second Viscount Chichester, is memorialised. The viscount wears his coronet but only his second wife has hers: his first wife, Dorcas, died before he had his inheritance. His second wife is shown with her stillborn child with whom she died in 1648. The monument celebrates the viscount's military associations and at Lady Mary's feet are five sons and two daughters, all of whom pre-deceased their parents. This composition is the only one of its kind in Devon. There is an eeriness to it: two children hold hands, another rests his hand on his brother's head. James, Digby, Arthur, Edward, Beatrix, Arthur and John line up in a tidy row. They have faces similar to the angels carved at the top of the columns. See **Holcombe Rogus** for the effigy of the viscount's sister.

In the north wall of the chapel Edward, first Viscount Chichester of Carrickfergus and his wife Anne lie on their funeral bed. Their son Arthur erected the monument and there are similarities with the coronets. He wears a viscount's coronet but she is without because Lady Anne died before he was ennobled. Chichester lived nearly a generation after her death. There are traces of original colour on the white marble. He inherited substantial property in Ireland which was then being colonised and Eggesford, as remote from the sea as any Devon parish, must have seemed far removed from Irish affairs.

In the east end of the chapel is a third monument which catches the eye. This massive collection of marble dates from the early eighteenth century and demonstrates the change in taste to classical imagery. A vase and four figures have disappeared and this gives the monument a somewhat empty look. There are other memorials of less interest dotted around. One in the north west corner is unremarkable except for the deceased's name,

EDWARD, FIRST VISCOUNT CHICHESTER

Lady Urania Annabella Wallop. Near her is a memorial to Newton Wallop who changed his name to Fellowes in order to inherit. His memorial declines to note he was 'tremendously hammered' by a neighbouring vicar in a boxing match. It may have provided some comfort to him when he heard the Reverend William Radford described as the best boxer then in Devon.

It is worth noticing that the basin of the font is Norman with decorated sides. There is also some glass, most of which is from the nineteenth century (see Ilfracombe for the same angels) but some earlier fragments survive, notably the head of the Virgin Mary and possibly Jesus, in the tower window. Notice also the Tortoise Stove with the motto slow but sure combustion.

Although the monuments were erected in the keen wish to be remembered, they have not always been on show. Through the 1840s the memorials were boarded up and other family monuments discarded. That short period in the early Victorian period demonstrates how fleeting fame can be.

⚷— *Open*

OPPOSITE: THE CHICHESTER MONUMENTS

17

ERMINGTON

ST PETER & ST PAUL
POSTCODE: PL21 9NS

The best known feature is, like Barnstaple, the leaning medieval stone needle-spire but it should be visited for one overriding reason, the craftsmanship of the Pinwell sisters.

When the church was restored in the 1880s the vicar's three daughters began making good the woodwork. These women went on to set themselves up in business in Plymouth before 1891 when they supplied Stoke Fleming with a pulpit. That year Mary, Annie and Violet Pinwell, then only 20, 18 and 17 years old, were listed in the census as living with their father but working as professional woodcarvers. Ten years later they were employing others. Violet continued to work as a carver until 1954.

This church has a pulpit carved by the sisters, its wooden and alabaster reredos (thought to have been after a Burne Jones design) was by Violet as is the Lady Chapel reredos and font cover. The Pinwells' work can be found throughout the South West (see **Lewtrenchard, Plympton St Mary**) but has been under-appreciated despite the obvious imagination and vigour of the carving. The church restoration was overseen by John Dando Sedding, architect, and his nephew Edmund Harold Sedding, ten years older than Violet and an architect, lived with the Pinwell family from at least 1891 to 1901. It was perhaps because of this connection that the Pinwell sisters were able to launch their woodcarving endeavour so successfully.

Some of the inventiveness of the Pinwells is shown by depicting their father, and the rest of the family including themselves, as angels at the base of the pulpit. Their carving has a lightness and delicacy, particularly noticeable in the poppy heads of the seating and with the reredos musical angels, which is lacking in the more solid woodwork being done elsewhere in Devon. Their work should be

THE PINWELL'S WOODWORK

DETAIL OF THE STRACHLEIGH TOMB

seen alongside that of other Victorian women who were then, before the Great War, supplying woodwork and stained glass to churches in Devon and further afield.

There are other fittings worth seeing. The seventeenth-century rood screen was called Grecian in the mid 1800s and renovated not long afterwards (including inserting new columns). The parclose screen is modern. A glimpse into the vestry shows a detailed sixteenth-century brass to the Strachleigh family. There is also an interesting tomb chest of the same date (now serving as an altar in the south aisle) with which were once associated two helmets (seen above). In 1866 Reverend Cresswell tried one on and found it the most uncomfortable head gear he ever had. At about the same time the Exeter Diocesan Architectural Society noted the monument as 'a warrior's tomb'. It has been painted since at least 1847.

The spider-web leads of the windows are out of the ordinary and can be found in other churches in the South Hams. Instead of creating designs from the glass the decoration lies with the shaping of the leads. The only Devon church to upstage Ermington for its leads is Lynton. When leaving the church it is worth noting the Great War cross beyond the impressive Arts & Crafts entrance gate.

⚷ *Open*

18

EXETER

ST MARTIN
POSTCODE: EX1 1EZ

Exeter once had several dozen small churches which filled the skyline with their red towers. St Martin's is a rare survival and it sits quietly in a corner of Cathedral Close, dwarfed by its great neighbour. Like the rest of Exeter the residents prayed in their own church rather than in the grand cathedral. It is remarkable that this building remains and that the interior survived Victorian renovation, wartime bombing and a long-vanished congregation.

The church is not detached like rural ones: only in Exeter were ancient parish churches built into adjacent properties. In this case it adjoins Mol's, an ecclesiastical building until the Reformation before it became the Elizabethan Customs House and later a Georgian coffee house run by women. St Martin's has no churchyard and its dead were interred either inside or in Cathedral Close. It is sited at a corner of the parish and a glance at the north side reveals a tortuous shape.

The entrance is through a west porch which was frequented on Christmas Eve by Georgians seeking hot curds and whey. Until the early 1800s the Close was gated and at night became an enclosed enclave. The church frontage runs broadly north to south but inside runs askew. It was consecrated a year before the arrival of the Normans, in 1065, and later building can be seen in the Beer stone windows which date from the late 14th or 15th centuries. Medieval glass is in the south windows including leering monsters. The thin tower is on the north. The church is rare in that it has its Anglo-Saxon plan as well as fabric in its rubble walls.

The gallery was erected sometime between 1689 and 1707. A quiet moment in the box pews, which were installed at this time, gives time to take in this tiny

church. To the right can be seen the Royal Arms of Charles I, dated 1635, and sometime afterwards the altar rails were installed. There are also benches in the chancel.

What is striking are the over-size monuments squeezed into a small church. This is particularly so with that to Philip Hooper who died in 1715. He paid for the nearby reredos which he looks away from. Hooper's body is oddly truncated, nearly dwarfish, and his most impressive feature is the flowing wig. Two oddly coloured books are placed at a variance and Hooper is not reading them, as is more common, but has a posture of upward devotional contemplation. On the cover of one is written the second sentence from 'The Order for the Burial of the Dead'. His angels are only partly dressed and misplaced their resurrection trumpets sometime in the last century. His memorial is by John Weston, one of Exeter's most illustrious masons.

To the left is a monument in newly glistening gold, to an Exonian who, we read, 'I perceive I have in all my life been walking to this grave'. The cherubs, two of the more than two dozen representatives of the angelic host in the church, rest with their spades.

THE WAKEHAM MONUMENT

The tower has two monuments from the long-demolished church of St Paul. One is to Sir Edward Seaward, a leading citizen and prominent Whig merchant. At the crown two well-fed putti hold up a breast-feeding pelican but at the base two small boys, equally well-nourished, present the emblems of Seaward's service. One has the scales of justice as well as the Roman symbol of authority in the bundle of wooden rods with an axe blade. The other has a broken column (to denote a premature death) and a horse's bridle. The column and fasces are modestly placed, hopefully without any other visual intent. The other memorial illustrates subsequent style: the deceased, seventeen-year-old Eliza Mary Mortimer, is taken to heaven by an angel.

By the early 1800s the church was dilapidated. The aspects of interest today had become old-fashioned and dull: the city's leading Victorian historian wrote 'nothing challenges attention' except the West Window. Since 1995 the church has been carefully cared for by the Churches Conservation Trust.

⚷— *Open*

OPPOSITE: THE CHANCEL AND DETAILS OF THE MONUMENTS

19

HACCOMBE

ST BLAISIE
POSTCODE: TQ12 4SJ

Haccombe has a distinct presence and is unlike any other church in Devon. Its position, in a secluded valley adjacent to the great house of the Carews, helps define the church but its rural isolation is misleading for there once was a village along the road leading to the church. The cottagers were removed as they interfered with the view from Haccombe House. As charming as its position is, it is the interior that marks out the church.

Haccombe was a collegiate church and shortly after its consecration in 1328 it had five chaplains and an Archpriest. It still retains that office. The church had restoration in the 1820s by John Kendall, who worked at Exeter Cathedral, and then a generation later by John Hayward, who was busy throughout the diocese. One curiosity is the horseshoe on the front door. This was widely known as that of the winner in a wager between two medieval gentlemen on who could ride his horse further into the sea. Another oddity is the partial retention of two arms carved in stone. Were these used for holding lights?

The red and white coloured interior may feel medieval but it is the sensitive work of John Kendall in the east end that helps maintain the atmosphere. The Beer stone reredos, stone chancel screen and pulpit are all by him as may be the choir stalls. This provides a pleasing background for some of the other important items although public opinion was outraged in 1851 by the placing of the Carew arms on the reredos.

The collection of thirteenth to fourteenth-century monuments is outstanding. There are two ladies, one with a book and the other with what is probably a heraldic shield, and a cross-legged knight grasping his sword. Note the residual colours and faintly staring eyes. Two others rest in the north aisle: Sir Hugh and

Lady Philippa Courtenay are at prayer on a chest tomb. Beside them is the most notable monument of all: a boy finely carved in alabaster barely two feet long has his head supported by angels and a heraldic beast (a dog?). The cushions and angels' wings still have colour but the beast's base gives the false appearance that the boy was once vertical and not always lying on his back.

SIR HUGH AND
LADY PHILLIPPA COURTENAY

There are five brasses dating from the late fifteenth century to the middle of the seventeenth. The number is possibly a record for a Devon church and each one commemorates the Carew family. They complement the stone effigies: Sir Nicholas Carew is in armour as is his relation Thomas. Maria and Elizabeth Carew are also depicted in brass but it is that for Thomas and Anne Carew which is truly remarkable. They died two days apart in 1656 and are surrounded not only by their six children but by death motifs: death's-heads, spades, scythes, bones, hourglasses and half-dressed angels.

There is more to notice on the floor. This church is remarkable for its collection of inlaid early fourteenth century (brown and yellow) tiles and a few early sixteenth-century Majolica tiles made in Seville. This group is the best in Devon.

The glass is also outstanding. That for the medieval period was reassembled in the 1800s, as was much of that elsewhere in Devon. There are several figures, of the fourteenth century, including Mary with the holy spirit and the Annunciation. In the south east window and in roundels in three windows are depicted John the Baptist (dated 1661) and there is also a version of Annibale Carracci's early-seventeenth century 'The Dead Christ Mourned' which is in the National Gallery. The Exeter firm of Beer supplied some later glass in 1846.

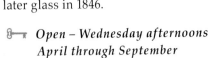 *Open – Wednesday afternoons*
April through September

ABOVE LEFT: SOME EARLY TILES
BELOW LEFT: MEDIEVAL GLASS

20

HARTLAND

ST NECTAN

POSTCODE: EX39 6DU

If Devon has corners then St Nectan's is in one of them. This church seems remote even from the village. It is one of Devon's most impressive churches and has nearly the tallest tower. The character is the result of it being one of the largest parishes, of being a collegiate church from 1050 and having been situated near a new Augustinian abbey a century later.

The churchyard is full of slate gravestones and it is hard to imagine its appearance in 1838 when the vicar deliberately let the grass grow high. Reverend Hawker wrote that his neighbouring cleric 'cherishes for his horse the grain that grows from out the bosoms of the dead'.

St Nectan's is spacious, airy and feels its age. Much of it dates to the fourteenth and fifteenth centuries but there were restorations in the middle of the nineteenth century and just before the Great War. Miss Creswell wrote a century ago that it was 'simple, yet bare, decorated but not gaudy'. She was right.

The medieval wagon roofs are impressive and the bosses in the Lady Chapel are particularly interesting. There are many plain seventeenth-century benches which are easily overlooked as are the earlier ones in the south chapel.
What takes the eye is the fifteenth-century screen which stretches across eleven bays. The ancient colours are still there. The leading expert on screens called it 'truly magnificent'.

Of equal interest is the Norman font near the tower. The carved decoration is rich but what is particularly remarkable are the four faces at each corner that look up to the bowl and the other four which leer down at them. Are these monsters, demons or men? Reverend Hawker of Morwenstowe is said to have thought this

represented the righteous looking down upon the wicked but if so hopefully godliness brings a benefit other than beauty. In 1938 the Emperor of Abyssinia admired the font but what he thought of the carvings is not known.

The medieval pulpit is easily overlooked as it is dwarfed by so much else and in the museum over the north porch are the remains of its Jacobean replacement. In 1625 a local man was paid to paint King James's name on the pulpit and those panels can be seen there today. In this room, called Pope's Chamber, are also some of the original nave roof panels. Reverend Hawker supposed that this was a monk's cell ('there dwelt Thought as a demon and Memory arrived garbed as a fiend. Long years, long years – the vigil of the night, the abstinence of the day, the solitary yell...') and a miserable one at that.

Some interesting items were brought from the abbey. In the chancel is a forbidding but ornately carved altar tomb of the late 1300s that was used as an altar and communion table from 1848 until 1931. It came during St Nectan's Victorian restoration. Previously it was used as a flower planter. There are fourteenth-century stone fragments in the south chapel: one angel has been decapitated but enough has survived of a couple holding hands to show how finely carved they were. Another figure is at prayer but the stone is deteriorating and the detail is being lost.

The glass is underappreciated and currently out of fashion. The most striking was installed in the early 1930s to illustrate the history of St Nectan's and they were praised at the time for the light they threw on the screen. There are five windows by the eminent stained glass artists Caroline Townshend and Joan Howson who were nicknamed 'The Citizens'; the two were Suffragettes, business and life partners and operated from Putney. Their glass reflects the early twentieth-century enthusiastic romanticism for medieval Britain and even includes Alfred and his cakes. The inspiration was Richard Pearse Chope, the leading antiquarian in Hartland. In the north chapel are three early roundels, that of the

Nativity is particularly detailed and interesting for a continental interpretation of the birth of Christ. The east door has two medieval monks carved as angels.

🗝 *Open*

LEFT: DETAIL OF EARLY TWENTIETH-CENTURY GLASS

OPPOSITE:
TOP LEFT: OUTSIDE THE WEST DOOR
TOP RIGHT: DETAIL OF THE SCREEN
CENTRE LEFT: SOME OF THE FIGURES FROM THE ABBEY
BOTTOM LEFT: THE NATIVITY ROUNDEL
BOTTOM RIGHT: ONE OF THE FONT'S FACES

21

HAWKCHURCH

ST JOHN THE BAPTIST
POSTCODE: EX13 5XD

There are two exceptional reasons to visit this church: it has the most surprising collection of Norman carving in Devon as well as fantastic Early English sculpture. A pair of binoculars is useful in many churches but they are essential for a successful visit to St John's. These carvings are largely unknown and part of the reason is that Hawkchurch lies along the border with Dorset and only became part of Devon in 1896. It is also not within the Exeter Diocese but of Salisbury. It has escaped the attention it deserves.

St John's was built in the twelfth century but had substantial restoration in 1862. In 1837 it was claimed that there were carvings of satyrs, nymphs and dwarves but these cannot be found today or were badly described. Fortunately the Victorians kept a good number of the carvings. The twelfth-century nave was then improved by a clerestory and the early corbel table of carved heads was moved to the north and south exterior walls. Those on the north have had more weather damage than their counterparts on the south wall. These are more easily seen, partly due to the direct sunlight, and comprise 22 carvings of various types. A few are geometric. The others include a ram (similar to one at **Branscombe**), possibly a lion, a number of demons, men with moustaches and a cleric (is he a bishop?) holding a book and crook. There are three couples. One pair holds hands while another have theirs below them. She smiles while he looks decidedly miserable. The third couple appears at a distance to be a man with a hump back but it could be a woman holding onto a hatted man's moustache who is looking away. Those carvings made of Ham stone, which are yellow, are Victorian copies while the rest are of a local limestone and are original. The two figures on the far right, in

THE RAM AND GOAT

the yellow Ham stone, are less clearly identified as they have had considerable weathering. They could be two conjoined animals.

Inside the church it is much easier to see other carvings of a different nature. These are later (Early English) than those along the roof. The church has round piers with capitals full of interesting details. One has a goat and ram playing musical instruments. There are also depictions of a man feeding a goose and another feeding what may be a dog or possibly a cat. Another figure, with a hood, is interacting with what looks like a squirrel. There are remnants of red colour on his tail. There are small corner figures in both aisles and one column has a figure which could be a monkey. Are there similarities here with Wells Cathedral?

In the chancel, at the base of a twelfth-century column, are two fighting dragons. Above is a green(ish) man with the end of a fantastic figure in his mouth. This long thin creature, one of several, looks like it was influenced by Viking art.

Ancient colour can be seen in crevices throughout these carvings which give a hint as to how they once looked. It is easy to become complacent about carvings but it is humbling to think they have been part of St John's for nearly nine hundred years and little appreciated outside of it.

⚷ *Open*

22

HIGH BICKINGTON

ST MARY
POSTCODE: EX37 9AX

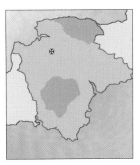

ɦigh Bickington is largely an unknown village. Even Professor Hoskins in his great work, *Devon*, found little to say but he recognised the church was of exceptional interest.

The arrival at the south door is extraordinary. This Norman doorway has a complicated series of carved rounded arches and on the left is a corbel head (see the space for another on the right). There is some ancient colour left on the doorway. Inside there is a piscina of the same date, a pillar with a cushion capital. Of greater interest is the font, it has a highly decorated bowl with semi-circular faces of inscribed wheels, rosettes and crosses.

However, the outstanding feature of this church is its ancient carved wood which one writer in 1849 repeatedly described as handsome. St Mary's is known for this collection of several score of fifteenth and sixteenth-century bench-ends which must be sought out throughout the church. The earlier ones have heraldry, saints and tracery patterns while the later ones are Renaissance designs such as individual portraits and foliage. There is one famous bench-end: the figure which looks like a monk at prayer was called Athelstone by local people.

There are also benches with carved (and defaced) tops. There is a legacy of all sorts of woodwork. Part of a later box pew survives and this has a carved panel on its door. The Victorian choir stalls also incorporate early woodwork and there is a bench-end suggested to be from the thirteenth century. The communion table is also worth an investigation as is the Victorian reredos with its reused panels possibly from a former screen. An iron parish chest recycles wood possibly from the seventeenth century. Notice the rector's name. There is also an earlier chest

THE NORMAN DOORWAY

THE SEATING AND DETAIL OF THE CARVING

'ATHELSTONE'

possibly made in the thirteenth century. The detail of the carving throughout the church demands attention: there are inventive portraits, grotesques, strange animals and well-fed cherubs playing musical instruments.

The interest in woodwork continued into the twentieth century. A local resident, Siddie Penny, carved two extraordinary frontals in the chancel. These have a procession of animals, some pass a pyramid, which even includes an American turkey. They are worthy successors of the superb ancient wood. There is also a Victorian octagonal pulpit which was removed from Exeter in the Second World War. With all this woodwork, and more which has not been described, it would be easy to miss the fifteenth-century wagon roof with its chamfered ribs and carved bosses. In the churchyard was a gravestone to Elizabeth Letheren. It refers to her as 'worms' meat'. A visit to High Bickington may be unusual for many Devonians but it will be memorable.

Open

23

HOLCOMBE ROGUS

ALL SAINTS
POSTCODE: TA21 0PE

This church sits alongside Holcombe Court and the lives of the former squires continue to dominate it. The Bluett family pew and chapel are the main reasons to visit; both are tremendous experiences.

The early seventeenth-century pew is unusual for Devon partly because it is a large separate space reserved for a gentry family but mostly for its flamboyance. Along the crest, on three sides, are fifteen carved medallions of biblical scenes. They are, from left to right, 1 a scene which has not been identified, 2 Adam & Eve under the tree, 3 Adam & Eve expelled from the Garden of Eden, 4 Adam ploughing the fields, 5 Adam & Eve with two children but Miss Cresswell thought it 'a happy pre-Adamite family', 6 Cain & Abel, 7 the sacrifice of Abraham, 8 Abraham and Melchisedeck, 9 Moses and the copper snake, 10 Moses and the burning bush, 11 Moses in battle with Aaron and Hur, 12 Balaam and the Angel, 13 Moses and the golden calf, 14 the Ark of the Covenant, and 15 spies carrying grapes from Canaan. The last two medallions were carved by a local man for the restoration of 1858. There have been other changes: in 1828 James Davidson found it had angels at the corners and in the centre was a figure of King David holding his harp. Even so, there is little to compare it with in Devon except for that at Alwington.

The fifteenth-century parclose screen was brought from Tiverton in 1854 and is known as the Walrond Screen. It has Tiverton merchants' mark. There also are some remaining panels of the church's own original screen which have been incorporated into the Bluett Pew.

Adjacent to the Bluett Pew is the family chapel. Two early seventeenth-century monuments dominate. Two centuries ago Devon's leading writer on

RICHARD AND MARY BLUETT

the Picturesque Movement thought these were 'of considerable beauty and magnificence'. The memorials were made of a mixture of East Midlands alabaster, marble and freestone. On the left is that to Sir John and Lady Elizabeth, who rest on their death bed with their eight daughters lined up below. Some hold skulls to indicate an early death. Richard and Mary Bluett are memorialised on the right in a monument made twenty years earlier. This may have been carved by the same mason who created the monument to Judge Glanville at **Tavistock** which has the same angry lion. Unusually Richard Bluett's eyes are open and focused on his wife below him. Her effigy is of a higher quality than his and it may be relevant that he died after her. The text notes not only her qualities but that she was the sister of Arthur Viscount Chichester (see **Eggesford**).

In the chapel and throughout the church are good memorial slates on the floor. Some have curiously-carved putti, not all retain their modesty. The stained glass is also worth investigating including the spectral image of Lazarus raised from the dead at the Crucifixion. The crowd is particularly animated as Mary Magdalene weeps.

🗝 *Open (Bluett Chapel open by arrangement)*

24

HOLNE

ST MARY
POSTCODE: TQ13 7SL

There is something fulfilling about St Mary's. It may be due to Dartmoor hanging just over the village or to the surprise one feels when coming into the church after what is a fairly uninspiring approach. The atmosphere is welcoming and the interior has a richness despite the preponderance of granite. This is despite Holne being what was described in 1831 as a 'retired village'. It still is but the meaning has changed.

The gem of the church is, in the words of a Georgian visitor, the 'handsome chancel screen... carved in oak, gilded and painted' *(see page 106)*. It stretches across the width of the building. There has been a recent restoration and the colours gleam, particularly those of the figures along the wainscoting. Shockingly, Pevsner described them as *'of no merit'* and the Exeter Diocesan Architectural Society noted the screen in the mid 1800s as *'poor'*. There is a delicate charm in the figures and a surprising range of faces, some of which are in clusters. A few have been defaced. The birds in the coving are erratic. The pulpit is also carved of wood and of the same date, c.1500 (the EDAS in contrast to its opinion of the screen thought the pulpit *'fine'*). The carving is rich and varied and the colouring is just as opulent and there are armorial shields at the feet of the vicar. Most of Devon's churches would have looked like this in the early 1500s but in Holne we can dispense with imagination.

In the North Transept is a window to Charles Kingsley who was born in the vicarage. Neither his Water Babies nor Westward Ho! are represented but there is a superb portrait of him. His side burns are finely drawn and there are worry lines on his forehead. The subject of the glass is the arrival of the three kings. The

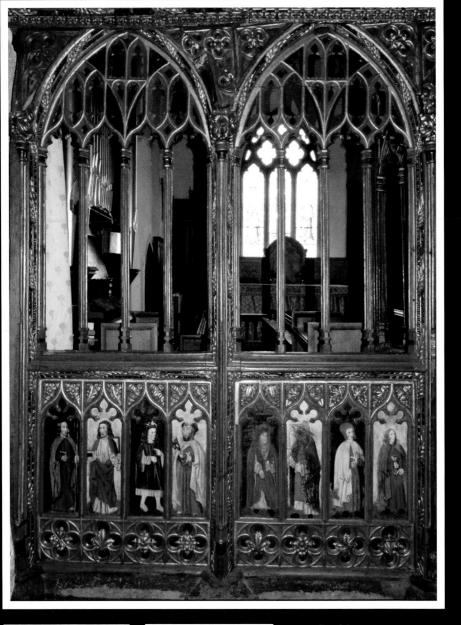

ABOVE: THE WOODEN SCREEN
LEFT: DETAILS FROM THE
PAINTED PANELS

OPPOSITE:
TOP LEFT: KINGSLEY
TOP RIGHT: ONE OF THE THREE KINGS
BOTTOM: THE PULPIT

detail is superb particularly that in the faces. Kingsley felt passionately about Dartmoor and throughout his life longed to return. He has.

In the South Transept is one of Devon's few original wooden crosses used to mark British graves from the Great War. It was, presumably, brought back once the Imperial War Graves Commission began replacing the first markers. It is also worth taking a moment to appreciate the great carved piece of timber that runs above the rood screen through into the north transept. Devon has few churches with wooden arches. It would be interesting to know the age difference between that beam and the ancient yew in the churchyard which has been hollowed out by time and resembles drunken friends propping each other up.

⚷ *Open*

107

25

ILFRACOMBE

HOLY TRINITY
POSTCODE: EX34 8BZ

Victorian Ilfracombe was a boom town and in 1877 one visitor compared it to a fascinating woman, 'its charms steal upon one unawares, by degrees'. Two Anglican churches were built to accommodate the growing population but the main church remained Holy Trinity. Tourism was the overriding money-maker and even the church was drawn into the industry. On the exterior is a shameless advert promoting local health-giving qualities: two slate stones are fixed to the east wall and advertise ten centenarians of the eighteenth and nineteenth centuries.

This is a large church with four aisles, a north tower and its windows are filled with stained glass. The church notes are the most comprehensive guide to the glass particularly given recent changes. It is a sumptuous collection of varied and vivid glass which should be appreciated window by window. There are bold and imaginative colours, some angels are sweet and precious while others have a restrained use of colour, and in several windows locals are portrayed.

There is an unusual slab stone of 1634 (by the south door) with highly decorative details and two seventeenth-century monuments with the medallions that North Devon specialised in (see **Barnstaple**). The war memorial has the grandest approach of any in Devon. The font is Norman and the pulpit with its arcaded decoration is Elizabethan.

There is much to find in this church but the most curious of all lies high above the congregation and just below the wagon roofs. These were renewed in 1899 but the corbels below them are far older and have been *in situ* since at least 1832. Two dozen figures run along the line of the nave. Some are engaged in acts which are not particularly polite. Miss Beatrix Cresswell, writing a century ago, thought they

108

A MODERN ANGEL

ANGELS AT THE NATIVITY

were *'the most weird collection of monsters that ever found their way into a sacred building.'* She dated them to the fourteenth century when Bishop Stapledon rebuilt the church (1321). They are comparable to figures at the base of Brixham's font which is thought to have been carved in the early 1300s. In the mid 1800s the Exeter Diocesan Architectural Society termed the Ilfracombe figures *'grotesque and curious animals'*. Another visitor, at about the same time, not only thought them unique but very fine in terms of craftsmanship and design. Moreover, he felt they should make the church famous. That fame has eluded the church so far.

There are 28 figures and possibly they were once arranged in pairs. Some are now incomplete. These are a mixture of grotesques, mythological creatures and animals. A view with the use of binoculars reveals some had one or two holes in their heads. Were there horns once? It is tempting to think that some illustrate

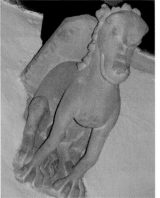

EARLY FOURTEENTH CENTURY FIGURES

evil and vice but others are friendly and cheerful figures. Some bare their teeth in friendly poses while others are decidedly not approachable. Perhaps the two most surprising figures are the male and female who are pleasuring themselves. One has a figure with an expression of either intense pain or ecstasy.

The angels above them are copies of original carvings. They were done by Gussie Hoskins, a local man, in the restoration of 1861. Cresswell also noted that in the early 1900s she could still see painted medallions between the arches of the nave. They had, she thought, evolved. Apparently one over the pulpit read *'How dreadful is this place'*.

⚷ *Open*

26

KENTISBEARE

ST MARY
POSTCODE: EX15 2AD

A unique feature of the church is apparent on first approaching the building: the tower, late fourteenth century or early fifteenth, has a striking chequerboard pattern made from the white Beer stone and the red sandstone from near Cullompton. Around the base is one of the most extensive collection of historic graffiti for a Devon church, some of it dates from the late 1700s. Several ancient yews are in the churchyard and at the entrance to the porch, on the left, is a tomb chest with a carved angel and death's-head.

St Mary's was described as being in 'a state of `woeful dilapidation' in the mid 1800s although that cannot be said today. The interior is dominated by two features, the screen and gallery. The screen has been described as one of the finest in the country and considered to be the prototype of what has been termed the 'Exe Valley type' of screens. Ten bays, each different, stretch across the width of the church and have flamboyant elements with good detail. According to the leading expert of screens, 'for variety of design and vigour and delicacy of execution, the work seems unequalled'. The screen also has the arms of John Whyting who died in 1529, built the South Aisle and whose tomb chest lies in his chapel. This monument was also made partly of Beer stone and is missing some of its heraldic brasses since they were stolen and thought to be taken to America in 1857. Whyting and his wife Anne may be depicted at the base of the drip-stones of the exterior of a north window: he is bearded and hatted while she wears a high headdress.

The gallery is dated 1632 and has rhyming verses (dismissed as 'doggerel rhymes' in the mid 1800s) to its erector, Mrs Anstice Wescombe, along with painted

One of Devon's finest screens

decoration and a series of neat wood carvings. Note one face is more akin to a Native American than the famous bench-end at East Budleigh. Another date mark shows the gallery was modified in the early 1700s.

The Whyting chapel, like the north chapel at nearby **Plymtree**, has domestic panelling. It may have originated from nearby Bradfield House. Other features in the church could be overlooked including the capital of one pier which not only has woolsacks with Whyting's mark but also the arms of the Merchant (Ad)Venturers of London as well as a ship. This is similar to **Tiverton** and **Cullompton** and shows the importance of the cloth trade to Devon.

Details of four memorials are interesting. In the Whyting chapel can be found a brass to Lady Mary Guildeford who died in 1558. On the north wall is a death's-head with the wings of a bat (unusual for Devon). Another on the same wall has one of Sir Walter Scott's last poems: lines written to commemorate his cousin who died of scarlet fever in 1830 at the age of 26. The south wall remembers the charity of Robert & Anstice Wescombe, whose initials are on the Gallery. The inside text details their gifts of more than £100 to the poor and Anstice also purchased the nearby, and extraordinary, Church House for the poor. It is now called Priesthall and can be seen outside the north-west corner of the churchyard. The Wescombe memorial's surrounding framework includes their two alabaster portraits, with fading and peeling paint, and above them a flaming heart shining with divine light on top of what could be the bible.

⚷━ *Open during the summer and at weekends in the winter*

A CARVING FROM THE GALLERY

THE BRASSES

27

LEWTRENCHARD

ST PETER

POSTCODE: EX20 4NU

The interest in this church lies not in its medieval origins but entirely in its re-creation by Sabine Baring-Gould who was both rector and squire from 1881 until his death in 1924. The church is one Victorian's very personal, if not idiosyncratic, renewal of an ancient building.

Baring-Gould is known within Devon for his antiquarian writings, his collecting local folk songs and for writing the words to '*Onward Christian Soldiers'*. However, throughout St Peter's can be seen a wider interest: the building demonstrates his now-forgotten cosmopolitan upbringing and personal taste. Baring-Gould collected an odd mixture of items from Belgium (the medieval triptych and chandelier), France (the sixteenth-century eagle lectern), Germany (the early twentieth-century East Window) and Switzerland (the late Victorian altar painting).

SBG inherited his uncle's estate, and church, and set about embellishing the church including removing the mustard yellow pews which had recently been inserted. As a younger man SBG had saved nine of the ancient benches that his uncle had removed and these can be seen today including several with good medallion portraits, another depicting a fool and a third showing St Michael the Archangel victorious over Satan and in the midst of weighing souls. In the mid 1800s the Exeter Diocesan Architectural Society described this as a grotesque carving and that he was '*the angel of judgment with sword and balance leading a dragon'*. There are also early sixteenth-century panels, possibly not originally from the church, which were reused for the clergy stalls.

The greatest introduction is undoubtedly the screen. His uncle had dismantled the screen but SBG had found portions in the tower, a wood shed and in the

Top: The screen

Lower picture arrangement:
Details of the early benchends
and two of The Pinwell's demons

Devon's Fifty Best Churches

MEMORIAL OF SUSANNA WILLIAMS, 1758

lumber room of the manor house. He had a new screen built in 1899 using these fragments for inspiration and employed his cousin, Bligh Bond, the national expert on screens, as the architect. The work was carried out by the Pinwell sisters of Ermington. Some painting was done by another woman, SBG's second daughter Margaret.

The Pinwell Sisters, then a fabulous force in Devon woodcarving, were also responsible for the pulpit which was modelled on that at Kenton. Three odd, if not demonic, figures can be found almost hidden away by the windows.

Another disturbing figure is that of a Victorian child who sleeps in a recess in the south chancel. It is also German and depicts Beatrice Baring-Gould. Notice the cup with the inscription *'Think on Me'*. The church has a series of some 15 early slate memorials to the Gould family which were removed, that is rescued, by SBG from Staverton Church in 1877. As interesting as these are, there are also 'Folk Art' slate stones of the 1700s outside (the best lie to the west and east of the church). One memorial has even been placed above the door, since at least 1849, where a sundial traditionally would be positioned.

⚷ *Open*

BEATRICE BARING-GOULD

28

LITTLEHEMPSTON

ST JOHN THE BAPTIST
POSTCODE: TQ9 6LY

This church stands quietly at the end of the village and its greatest disturbance has probably been the rowdiness of the navvies when they built the railway to Plymouth in the 1840s. Many thousands of Great Western travellers have had a quick glimpse but far fewer visit and see its treasures.

There are a number of reasons to make a trip to Littlehempston. A local red sandstone font, carved into seven sides and with ribs along the underside, still sits in the church. The rood and parclose screens are worth anyone's attention: the detail is good, the carving delicate and there is some early colour.

The church is light and cheerful, certainly more so than in the 1640s when the spectral Zachary Bogan was in the church. This local boy was a devoted Puritan who listed, in over 600 pages, the threats and punishments that the bible promised to sinners. Bogan began with Adultery and continued through to Whoremongering. He suffered from depression (`buried alive in melancholy' in his own words) and returned to Littlehempston during the Civil War. Bogan died at the age of 34 of consumption shortly after publishing his *Threats and Punishments*. He had spent years appearing as a 'walking skeleton' in the village.

The windows have been occupied by three medieval effigies since at least 1847. The earliest, of the early fourteenth-century, is a knight in armour, cross-legged and carrying his shield. He was carved in two halves and is missing most of his nose and part of his moustache but his eyes still look out. The second effigy has also been damaged. The lady dates somewhere between her two long-standing companions, at least in only one sense of the term, and her face is remarkably intact except for her nose.

LITTLEHEMPSTON'S THREE EFFIGIES

The surprise of the church is the late fifteenth-century glass. One Victorian writer has noted that this was not in the church until the mid 1780s when it was brought from Marldon. A Totnes glazier had been given the use of the glass to repair a window at Marldon from *'a rubbish heap full of glass in the belfry'*. He was allowed to keep any surplus with the condition that he cleared it out of the way of the bell ringers. The vicar of Littlehempston subsequently purchased the glass for ten pounds and gave one of the three panels to the provost of Oriel College in Oxford. Littlehempston has St Stephen standing on the left and St Christopher to his right. Beneath them are two pairs of devout donors who have nothing to do with Littlehempston other than that they have been resident here for some two hundred years. Fortunately although Georgian Marldon did not appreciate its medieval glass there was someone in Littlehempston who did.

Most visitors will not notice the star-shaped tracery at the apex of the fifteenth-century windows (of the chancel chapels and the north chancel window), an architectural detail found in Littlehempston and in only a few other Devon churches in the South Hams including Torbryan.

⚷ *Open*

OPPOSITE: THE GLASS IS THOUGHT TO HAVE ORIGINATED FROM MARLDON

29

MORTEHOE

ST MARY MAGDALENE
POSTCODE: EX34 7DU

I n 1832 Mortehoe was described as 'a poor bleak village on the coast but is occasionally visited during the summer season by tourists and invalids'. Since then it has been redefined by surfing but the parish church continues much as it has been over nine centuries. This is not a great or grand church filled with stunning fabric but is instead rather quiet and unassuming, overlooked by most of each year's thousands of visitors intent on finding the sea, but what it has is charm and an unusual collection of Pre-Raphaelite glass.

The glass is good, vibrant and oddly welcoming. There is an odd mixture here and like most glass it was donated as memorials. The oldest, only of the 1850s, is probably by Beer of Exeter: this is in the chancel and remembers Thomas Lee, an architect who drowned at age 38 while swimming at Mortehoe. Included is an architectural drawing of a church.

Another window features copies of Joshua Reynold's figures which are in Oxford's New College. Here we have two of the virtues, Faith and Hope. In another is a copy of William Holman Hunt's 'The Light of the World' of the 1850s. Interestingly, Hunt, a member of the Pre-Raphaelite brotherhood, rebelled against Reynolds. The glass to the left is another familiar Victorian image; it was inspired by a line in the hymn 'Rock of Ages' by Augustus M. Toplady, an eighteenth-century vicar in East Devon.

Two windows were given by the Ness family and both were designed by Henry Holiday, who was influenced by Burne Jones, a follower of the Pre-Raphaelites, and who was probably still in the employ of Powells when he created this glass. The colours are vivid and have a bold intensity which is lacking in Beer's windows.

SOME OF THE STRIKING GLASS AT MORTEHOE

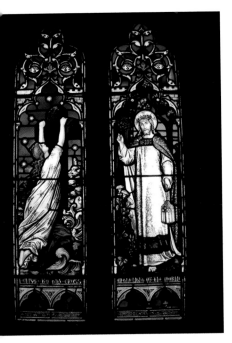

THE RUGGED CROSS AND THE
LIGHT OF THE WORLD

At the angle corner of the chantry are four windows to archangels Michael, Uriel, Raphael and Gabriel. These were by Selwyn Image who was responsible for the mosaic on the chancel arch of the ascending angels. Image gave up a career in the Church of England to become a designer of stained glass and in 1910 became Professor of Fine Art at Oxford. The mosaic was executed by the Powell firm. A century ago Miss Cresswell thought the donors had mistaken zeal in putting it in the church: she felt it looked out of place in a Gothic church.

One monument is significant. In the south transept lies a tomb chest of the early 1300s which was formerly attributed to William de Tracey, one of the murderers of Thomas a Becket. On the lid is an incised figure of a priest with a chalice. There are a series of figures within arches along the sides and at the end a panel depicting the Crucifixion. Interestingly, the figures look more worn than defaced and there are some bright traces of original colour. It was claimed in the early 1600s that some men had recently 'mangled' the tomb in a search for lead.

Worth noticing are the cheeky boys, not cherubs, climbing the wall monument to Mary and Thomas Newell. The classical development in monuments is seen with that to Mary Heddon. This was carved by Harry Hems and two angels bring Mary to heaven.

There are also early graffiti on one column. The benches are of a high quality but have few signs of age found in late medieval wood. They were restored around the turn of the twentieth century perhaps with a great deal of vigour. Miss Cresswell thought the West Gallery had protected them but it may have been box pews which shielded them from damage. She felt the 'weird collection of creatures are more suggestive of the visions of the nightmare than of any animals Adam might have named in Paradise'.

In the churchyard there is a gravestone to Robert Tucker who died in 1832.

> 'physicians aid was all in vain,
> No balsam could be found,
> Nor wife's kind love could not avail,
> To heal the mortal wound'

⌛ *Open during the summer and at other times by arrangement*

AFTER REYNOLDS

30

OTTERY ST MARY

ST MARY

POSTCODE: EX11 1DQ

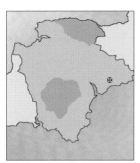

At first glance this church is so reminiscent of Exeter Cathedral that it appears to be a copy and is popularly known as a miniature version of it. St Mary's founder was an Exeter bishop who may have wanted future generations to remember the relationship between the two churches. He built a grand building, second only to the cathedral. Its two porches alone are more distinguished than some local churches. What makes Ottery even more fascinating is that in the early 1300s the church, with the master mason William Joy, was at the forefront of European design.

In 1328 John Grandisson was consecrated bishop of Exeter. Shortly afterwards he purchased Ottery manor from Rouen Cathedral, founded the collegiate church here and gave it, with the manor, to the warden and canons. Grandisson rebuilt an exisiting church and probably finished in the 1540s, before Exeter Cathedral itself was completed. His church was extended in the shape of a cross and has one spire as Exeter Cathedral had until the eighteenth century.

In 1520 a northern aisle was built by Cicely, Marchioness of Dorset. The *'Dorset Aisle'* enlarged the building but distorted the cruciform shape. Its fan vaulting is one of the most memorable features of the building. Only 25 years later the Reformation claimed the building: the college was dissolved and, like Crediton, governors were appointed and they remain nearly 500 years later.

Emerging from the south porch into the nave is a breath-taking view. The eye is taken upwards – partly distracted by modern repainting in patriotic colours – above the clerestory. The vaulting is magnificent. Eventually the visitor gazes at floor level and two fourteenth-century monuments emerge: one is to Sir Otho

THE SOUTH TOWER

Grandisson, the bishop's younger brother, and the second memorialises Lady Beatrix, his wife. Sir Otho rests in full armour and his long moustache trails well beneath his chin. The tiny face of Lady Beatrix is dwarfed by her headgear but she has the support of two angels, one of whom rests a hand on her shoulder.

A walk along the Dorset aisle is inspiring. The decorative capitals should not be missed, particularly the owls of Bishop Oldham and the wonderful elephant's head. At the north end is the partly-coloured monument of alabaster and marble to John Coke who died in 1632. Across from the North Transept is one of the gems of the church, the medieval clock with the sun and moon. The face is fifteenth-century.

There is so much to see but easily missed. The lectern, a gilded eagle, was presented by Grandisson. This is now in the Lady Chapel. The wooden parclose screens are from the 1300s and there are benches from the 1500s. The bosses are rich, the clerestory has stained glass designed by Pugin, the sedilia is curiously open at the back, and in the chancel is the Tudor monument to John Haydon of nearby Cadhay. He appropriated an Easter Sepulchre on which to site his memorial. Its situation may not be as odd as it first seems. He was a governor at the Reformation and took the place of the Catholic officials who would have been buried in this part of the building.

These are some early features but restorations and renovations in the 1800s, particularly by Butterfield did much to change the church.

OPPOSITE: Looking west in the Dorset Aisle
ABOVE: The Haydon monument

His font was built of marble from Ipplepen and Plymouth as well as serpentine from Helston in Cornwall. In 1869 one commentator disparaged the state of the church before it was refurbished: he noted *'to those who have ever seen it no words are wanted'*.

More recently the church has been associated with the Coleridge family. In the 1700s Reverend John Coleridge read the bible in Hebrew to farm workers. The hand of Grandisson is more easily seen today but it is worthwhile to pause and consider what it was like 250 years ago for agricultural labourers to have a cleric instruct them in Hebrew, 200 years after the Reformation opened up the bible to their ancestors with English.

⚷ *Open*

31

PAIGNTON

ST JOHN THE BAPTIST

POSTCODE: TQ3 3AH

The English Rivera is unknown here. This is old Paignton, a coastal village which for centuries engaged in fishing, farming and trade. There is a tranquillity here not found in the entertainments below. Nearby is a similar tower of local red stone from the adjacent Bishop's Palace. This would made an impressive ecclesiastical quarter.

The entrance is now via the Norman archway, an attractive mix of red and white stone with three distinct orders of moulding. There is a Norman font, returned in 1930 after being given away, and also a fifteenth-century cadaver. However, the distinguishing feature here is the chapel of the Kirkhams. One illustrious Edwardian commentator thought it *of almost unrivalled beauty and delicacy*. It has had considerable damage. In 1828 it was said 'barbarism has been suffered to riot with impunity' but some harm may be unintended: particularly vulnerable stone work has been broken as well as carving near seating.

However damaged, mutilated and defaced it is, the sculpture is overwhelmingly impressive and a remarkable survival for a fifteenth-century Catholic chantry chapel. It is unusual in having twin tombs separated by a doorway. The visitor passes between two couples (in miniature) who lie at rest within a wide stone screen. Below are a dozen figures, now headless, on both the north and south faces. The north side has male figures and the south are female. The only exceptions to this are the four evangelists.

The figures include apostles, other saints and mourners ('weepers'). Above them is miniature fan-vaulting and at the top are angels set among pinnacles. Every part is covered by imagery and ornament.

THE WEST DOOR

The Medieval pulpit

Within the internal side panels at the head and feet of the effigies the carving is particularly good. From the west there is the Visitation and facing it the Holy Family. That on the east shows Saints Roche and Anthony of Egypt while the facing panel is an extraordinary Mass of St Gregory (compare with **Ashton**). The figures have been interpreted as, from bottom left, a bishop, the pope, a cleric and above them two cardinals. The pope is gazing at a now nearly-vanished figure of Jesus: his right foot, left leg and left arm can still be seen. Clearly visible on the altar is a fringed cloth along with an open missal and two candlesticks. Some items have disappeared, including the bowl (did the blood of Christ pour into it?) but what is astounding is the survival of so many symbols of the Passion: Veronica still holds her cloth and there are three dice, a spear, nails, ladder, pincers and pieces of silver.

ST GREGORY'S MASS

The Kirkham family must have created the chapel but their original indications have gone. The painted dedication has been stripped away and even the heraldry on the shields no longer survives. It seems extraordinary that the individuals who made such an effort have had their own part obliterated.

The chapel also has a later tomb chest to Sir William and Lady Mary Kirkham. Here two Jacobeans face one another but now handless. In stone between them are two hearts entwined under a crown. Their effigies here, in a chapel close to other venerated sculpture, would have raised eyebrows but it probably once stood elsewhere. The couple were recusants and would have preferred their monument where it is now.

Near the chapel is the pulpit, a fifteenth-century stone wineglass-stem with headless saints and angels but the exuberant beasts have largely escaped that fate. Some original colour survives. The niches were once filled with plaster to disguise the figures.

There are other items of less significance but of great interest. The south porch is medieval and has an interesting boss. There is also some good nineteenth-century glass. The bright colours of the sedilia obscures its earlier origins: it was made up of older fragments. There is a door for dogs or was it for a cat? Near the chancel is a carved slate of rustic workmanship to the memory of Joan Butland who died in childbirth in 1679. Her son John was buried fourteen months later after pining a year for her.

⚷ *Open by arrangement*

32

PARRACOMBE

ST PETROCK

POSTCODE: EX31 4RJ

It is hard not to be bowled over by the charm of this church. Unlike its counterparts across Devon this building was not improved by the Victorians. The consequence is a visit feels like stepping back in time to a country church two centuries ago.

The church has an appealing plainness which will be better appreciated by the discerning visitor. Even in its day this was not a wealthy church but the fittings could appear to modern eyes as impoverished because we are more used to seeing Victorian embellishments, restorations and rebuilds with strong vivid colours. A visit to the replacement church in the village below shows what would have happened to St Petrock's church.

In the 1870s there was a proposal to demolish St Petrock's but the rector said *'instead of destroying its character by restoration we purpose to keep it repaired as a mortuary chapel'*. John Ruskin amongst others contributed a considerable sum and a new site for a modern church was found. The building however gradually declined and in 1971 was taken over by the Churches Conservation Trust.

There is a lack of colour except for a few set pieces and these have been recently restored and perhaps are more noticeable for it. But the overwhelming focus of the eye is on the wooden seating and stone columns; these are all plain and understated but have a richness and depth of colour all of their own. Ten minutes can be usefully spent on a bench or pew contemplating the church and it will also provide an appreciation of the comfort with which parishioners listened to a morning's sermon. Few visitors can last ten minutes on one of the wooden benches.

LOOKING EAST DOWN THE NAVE

THE SOUNDING BOARD

BENCHES WITH RAISED SEATS BEHIND

THE 'NEW' FONT

The chancel dates from the thirteenth century and the south porch may be from the sixteenth but the fittings themselves are mostly post-Reformation and nearly all are of the seventeenth or eighteenth centuries. There is a mix of benches and later box pews. Interestingly, those at the back are on tiers. Lady Northcote suggested in 1930 that the rood beam had been dismantled and the wood used to make the ends of the benches. This is hard to see today. Notice the peg hooks (see **Teigngrace**). In the midst of them is the font, possibly Norman, brought from Martinhoe Rectory in 1908 when Parracombe's tower was repaired after a lightning strike.

The pulpit is again not overly decorated but what is more conspicuous is the octagonal sounding board with the painted underside and the verse from 2 Corinthians 4:5. Notice the attached minister's reading desk and clerk's seat. Above them is the tympanum in wood. It has the Lord's Prayer, the Ten Commandments and Creed along with the Royal Arms of the Hanoverians. The screen below is simple, understated and a rare early example. Beyond it lies the communion rails with stick balusters. On the walls are three tablets carved in wood but (recently re-) painted to appear as if they were made of more expensive stone.

⚷— *Open*

33

PILTON

ST MARY
POSTCODE: EX31 1QT

St Mary's has an unusual main entrance, this is through an impressive range of Victorian almshouses. Their style harkens back to an earlier period and indeed the church itself had been part of a Benedictine priory from 925. The north side has the marks of the earlier monastic buildings. This is a great church, extensive in size and rich in its fittings.

There is a Georgian sundial of 1780 by John Berry on the south side and on the north lies the tower. In the south porch is the list of the more than 300 local men who served in the Great War (from the days when the bishop forbid the names of serving men to be inside the church itself).

The font is extraordinary not so much for it or the cover (which is good) but for the great canopied tester. This is an extravagant affair and has interesting fretwork including an angel and a devil below him. Unfortunately it has been painted white. Nearby is the medieval pulpit with a Jacobean sounding board and, most unusually, an arm for holding an hourglass (see **Tawstock**).

The screen is another marvel. It crosses ten bays and is elaborate in its carving. Some colour survives and the figures are unusual. Notice the one arm and hand within the cornices. The later parclose screen is just as rich and has the letter 'R' possibly for Raleigh, the home of the patrons of the church. There is also a sixteenth-century communion rail and table.

There are exuberant Elizabethan and early Stuart monuments to the Chichester family. That in the chancel to Sir Robert Chichester is particularly eye-catching because the figures are set at prayer and wear mournful expressions. Behind Sir Robert is his son and daughter and facing them are his two wives Frances and

The Chichesters

TWO OF THE CHICHESTER FAMILY

Mary and an adult daughter. These three women have the same face although their clothes slightly differ. Despite the dustiness of the figures and the need for some restoration the quality of the carving stands out.

Easily missed is the West window: a handsome Great War memorial by Blanchford of Exeter. It has unusual depictions of those who served including a VAD nurse.

Nearby see Marwood, five miles to the north, which also has exceptional woodwork

⚷ *Open*

DETAIL FROM THE GREAT WAR MEMORIAL WINDOW

34

PLYMOUTH

MINSTER OF ST ANDREW

POSTCODE: PL1 1DU

esurgem has been St Andrew's key word for 70 years. In 1941 the church was hit by German bombs, burnt out and then on the following morning a wooden board was discovered, on the north door, with this single Latin word *Resurgem* (`I will rise again'). This neatly identified the resurrection of St Andrew's with that of Christ.

For most of its Christian history Plymouth had only one parish church in which all attended services. In comparison Exeter was a city of several dozen (small) churches but Plymouth had this single great building, possibly the largest parish church in Devon. The tower stands at 136 feet.

St Andrew's is in two parts. Much is defined by its past. Medieval Plymouth was a prosperous port and the generations immediately before the Reformation built on a grand scale. The bombing destroyed the fittings but some monuments survived. Some are the filthiest in Devon possibly because of normal urban grime but no doubt enhanced by bomb-smoke and dust. The earliest (in St Philip's Chapel) is an effigy dated to before the church was built. There are two interesting ones of the early 1600s. A kneeling John and Deborah Sparke are at prayer with their family in the south aisle while Elizabeth Calmady (along the north wall) is also devout but she has an extremely crude monument. Her likeness and those of her children have been scratched into local stone. This was poorly done compared to others in Devon and particularly in Cornwall.

An early nineteenth-century monument by Richard Westmacott to Dr William Woollcombe features figures of Medicine and Charity along with a medallion portrait. His epitaph curiously notes he had a 'peculiar mildness and benevolence of his character'. Another to Reverend John Hatchard, vicar of St Andrews for 45

THE ASTOR WINDOW

IN THE SOUTH TRANSEPT

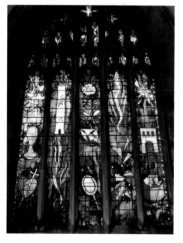

THE LADY CHAPEL WINDOW

years, has a cholera scene but his memorial has no reference to mildness. In fact his bust looks positively fierce. There are other monuments that have a likeness: there is a head by Sir Francis Chantrey of Zachary Mudge, an earlier vicar of the church, whose wig gives him the appearance of wearing ear muffs, and John Gandy, yet another of St Andrews' vicars, has a medallion portrait either by Chantrey or E. A. Lege as part of a more complicated assemblage illustrating his many and varied accomplishments but then again he was in post for 56 years. These three were the only vicars from 1732 to 1870, a total of 148 years.

These are interesting in themselves but the distinguishing feature of this church relates to its post-war past. The modern glass is vigorous, intense and attention-grabbing. It is the most exciting of Devon's modern glass and has a greater effect due to the lack of any competing glass in north or south windows. There are six on the east and west sides designed by John Piper and made by Patrick Reyntiens in the 1950s. They comprise 'Music & Inspiration' (North Transept); 'Symbols of the Virgin Mary', 'the Four Evangelists: Air, Earth, Fire & Wind', 'Catherine's Wheel and St Andrew's Cross' (East Windows); 'Creation and the Trinity' (South Transept) and 'St Andrew's Cross and Passion' (West Window). The vivid colours are in stark contrast to the grey granite columns and windows, the white walls and the grey wall monuments. The glass divides public opinion but they effectively proclaim the rebirth of the church. A useful comparison can be made with the glass at the Guildhall.

There is one particularly interesting relic of the Sea Dogs: below a window in the south aisle is graffiti scratched into the plasterwork. It has been suggested to be the arms of Sir Francis Drake. Some lines have been recently coloured but others can be seen which provide other patterns. Drake would have trouble recognising St Andrew's as would the Plymouth Pilgrims who would have visited briefly but this church, unlike many others bombed in the 1940s, had a resurrection.

⚷ *Open*

35

PLYMPTON ST MARY

ST MARY

POSTCODE: PL7 2AA

This church is under-appreciated and better known for the adjoining ruins of the Augustinian priory than for itself. St Mary's has much more to offer. Gargoyles, described as 'grotesque heads' in the early 1800s and as 'uncouth figures' in 1847, stare open-mouthed and bug-eyed along the south side. One Victorian preferred the north side's 'heads of monks with open mouths and protruding tongues'. The south porch is fifteenth-century and has three niches above the outside door. The middle figure probably once held a crucifix and a dove to depict the Trinity. The statues at each side look like devout donors but may be Mary and the Angel Gabriel. The vaulting inside is elegant despite not having a great deal of restoration. Christ is simply-carved and apparently beardless.

Much of the spacious interior is of the fifteenth-century (the piscina may even date to 1311 and has interesting colouring) and there is a chest tomb to an unknown man (possibly William Courtenay of Loughtor) of the 1460s. Decapitated mourners stand at the base while he rests in an imperfect state, noseless but with still an impressive head of hair.

In the north chapel is a similar chest tomb to Richard Strode of 1464. He wanted his monument to be below a new window dedicated to St Sidwell. This memorial has almost completely escaped the vandalism of its counterpart in the south aisle. He rests in a near perfect state (albeit his nose has had work) as do the figures below. The lack of mutilation is due to the monument having been partly buried until the 1830s when the floor was lowered. Eleven figures were revealed, presumably having been obscured through the Reformation. Some may be monks (first, third, fifth, ninth and eleventh) with the second figure being Saint Paul, the

THE WEST PORCH CEILING

THE UNDAMAGED FIGURES

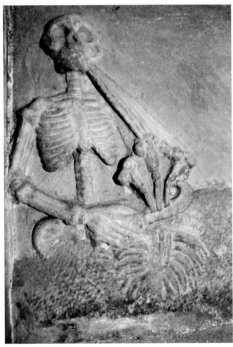

THE RISING SKELETON

fourth Saint Katharine, the sixth the Trinity, the eighth
Mary and the tenth Saint John the Evangelist.

A wall monument in the north chapel to Sir
William Strode of 1637 has an unusual depiction (for
Devon) of a skeleton rising out of the grave and cutting
a flower with his sickle. Ten children are depicted:
by his first wife Mary he had Richard, William, John,
Mary, Joanna, Ursula, Frances, Julian, Margaret and
Elizabeth. Strode was an M.P., puritan-minded and
both wives pre-deceased him

His third son John was 'the best bowler in all
England' but his second, William, gained more fame.
He was one of the five Parliamentarians imprisoned
in the Tower by King Charles in 1629. William was
incarcerated for twelve years and was held with such
respect by Parliament that upon his death he was

PINWELL'S WORK

interred in Westminster Abbey. At the Restoration he was viewed with equal
contempt by the Royalists, dug up and removed. The simple carving gives no
indication of his state when the monument was erected.

In 1829 local tradition related the elder William died quarrelling with a
neighbour over a trespassing peacock. A field was then still known as 'Peacock
Fond Meadow' while that in which Strode died was 'Man's Blood'. However, an
earlier family history, of 1719, recorded that an ancestor of Sir William died over
the peacock and that from it the name Peacock Ford was given at Marsh Mills. That
account asserts the duel occurred during the War of the Roses.

In the chancel is an uneasy memorial to eleven-year-old Viscount Borringdon.
He died after ingesting an ear of rye. It depicts a rose
borne down by an ear of corn. As unusual as this may
be, perhaps the oddest object is the 'Red Indian Chair'
allegedly carved by sailors. It was fashioned from
several distinct sources with four or five pieces being
considerably older.

Medieval glass fragments are in the north aisle,
including two figures. The later East Window is
a stunning composition which unfortunately is
partially obscured by a later vigorous reredos (in
commemoration of a vicar lost whilst climbing
in the Alps). Also in the chancel is some delicate wood
carving by the Pinwell sisters. Their work continued
their consistent stamp of imagination and elegance
including even spider webs.

Open for daily worship and by arrangement

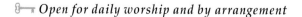

DETAILS OF THE EAST WINDOW

36

PLYMTREE

ST JOHN THE BAPTIST
POSTCODE: EX15 2JU

The arrival to the church is enhanced by the ancient yew tree on the south side and the impressive tower with its ancient statue of the Virgin Mary and Jesus on the west. In the 1930s the head of Jesus was found and put it in a safe place. It may still be there. The exterior is enjoyable (it was described in 1793 as one of the most beautiful in the deanery) but it is the interior which is truly delightful.

In 1892 one visitor was shocked at the state of the church. He wrote '*I was perfectly horrified to find with the tumble-down state of God's House, more so with the filth and dirt, the accumulation I should say of ages. which is absolutely inexcusable*'. Previous generations had directed funds towards a school building and not for church renovation. The legacy is the building has retained much of the older fabric.

The interior is filled with light, due to the paucity of coloured glass. A rustic collection box is sited near the west entrance but is easily overlooked for it sits amongst a great collection of fifteenth-century oak benches. Delicate tracery can be seen on the bench fronts while the ends have simple largely floral motifs set in two tiers. There are later benches, others were removed, but the nave is filled with what appears to be a complete set of ancient seats. Remarkable.

The sense of escape from modernisers is heightened when one realises the ceilings have retained their possibly seventeenth-century plaster vaults but the view of the nine-bay oak screen is overwhelming. The carving is delicate, ancient colour survives and the 34 base panels feature saints and New Testament figures including a rather forlorn Virgin Mary with an animated baby Jesus receiving the Three Wise Men. The vicar theorised these hose-wearing figures were Henry

THE ALABASTER CARVING

ONE OF THE RICHLY PAINTED FIGURES IN MEDIEVAL DRESS

VII, his son Prince Arthur and Cardinal Morton. Miss Cresswell thought this 'an ingenious inference of doubtful probability'. Box pews had covered some of the paintings: in 1918 one visitor recalled that some were mouldy.

Near the rood screen door is an image niche in the pier (there are others) but what lies beyond is unexpected. The sanctuary is lined with seventeenth-century wainscoting including a series of what are probably Flemish female figures and on the left two panels depicting the Crucifixion (notice the sun and moon) and an animated Nativity with the arrival of three shepherds. The panelling is thought to have come from a house pulled down in 1840 and the rector brought the carvings from Belgium in the mid 1800s. A glance at the other woodwork reveals an altar rail of the same date (with interesting cherubs) and more early bench-ends.

THE NATIVITY

The fifteenth-century font has a later cover ornamented by a bird, not gilded as in many other Devon churches. It is also unlike the once renown Plymtree Parrot, the remains of which were found in 1856 under the stone slabs of a local cottage and which local gossip conjectured were the vestiges of an unfortunate child. Here is also one of the great features of the church. Against the west wall is an alabaster panel previously part of the reredos also brought in by a Victorian cleric. It was there by the mid 1800s. This depiction of the Resurrection, dated to about 1600, is extraordinarily detailed. Roman soldiers have fallen asleep around Jesus still bearing signs of his crucifixion and to the right can be seen the arrival of three women to the tomb. In the bottom right-hand corner is a monstrous demon consuming a horned devil. Sublime seems too florid a word to describe it until one contemplates the skill with which it was carved. It may have been a gift of the same vicar who also gave 70 books to the Cullompton Mental Improvement Society, an overly-ambitious group which failed shortly afterwards.

Easily missed on the floor is a monument to a seventeenth-century couple whose marriage lasted 51 years and 10 months. It is also possible to step on the 700 year old floor tiles without noticing them...

THE SCREEN

⌚ *Open*

37
SHALDON

ST PETER
POSTCODE: TQ14 0DD

T his Arts & Crafts church promises little from the outside but the drabness of the exterior contrasts with the rich interior. It will only appeal to those who have a taste for simplicity in design and high quality materials. It will ether disappoint or delight.

The church was dedicated in 1902 and designed by Edmund Sedding (see **Ermington**) but local people seemed to have associated it more with the vicar: the implausibly-named Reverend Richard Marsh Marsh-Dunn gave the land (on which had stood an old coaching inn) and in 1920 he complained that local people dismissed it as his own personal church and not theirs. His unpopularity may have been due to his proposal that the local Great War memorial should be a new church roof. Shaldon voted and his suggestion came last. Interestingly the church war memorial is a crucifix, one of a handful in Devon and always indicative of leanings towards Anglo Catholicism. Bishop Ryle would not consecrate the church until the stone altar (theoretically illegal in the Church of England) was removed from the sanctuary and for several years it stood in the north aisle.

In 1892 the existing building on the land was partly pulled down and a temporary church was created out of the lower walls and a new corrugated roof erected. In 1899 work began on the new church.

Anyone with an appreciation of the Arts & Crafts movement will find the interior worth a visit although Miss Cresswell thought a century ago that the architect had a tendency towards 'the Flamboyant'. A superb west window, great variety of interior stone and surprisingly rich fittings all seek attention. The marble in the floor came from Devon, Italy and Africa and the building was constructed from local red stone as well as stone from Beer, Portland and Bath.

ABOVE: THE FONT
LEFT: THE CHANCEL, PULPIT AND ONE OF THE CARVED ANGELS

The pulpit is extraordinary, the rood screen one of the most elaborate in Devon and the font is equally unlike any other but oddly childlike as it is intended to depict John the Baptist. At the time it was pointed out that the saint is holding a clamshell, a native of North America with which he could not have been familiar. The marble angels in the chancel as well as the golden ones at the entrance to the Lady Chapel are worth inspection.

A visit to nearby Ringmore helps in appreciating the impact that this church had one hundred years ago. The chapel of St Nicholas had been the parish church. It was restored in 1894 (by Sedding) but the humbleness of the building stands in stark contrast to St Peter's.

⚷ *Open*

38

SHEBBEAR

ST MICHAEL
POSTCODE: EX21 5RU

The distinguishing feature of St Michael's lies at its entrance. Over the south door is an exceptional (for Devon) arch with floral decoration along the outside, beak-heads in the middle and zigzags at the bottom. Fifteen heads dominate the entrance and their beaks, noses or heads protrude over a cable. Although this mixture of animals and humans, and possibly demons, appears to owe more to the Mayans or Aztecs these are in fact Norman and they have gone green after some eight hundred years. Was this arch formerly in the church which has a nave and chancel dating back to the Normans? Less obvious in the arch are two additional heads at the head of the columns.

The interior is not a disappointment although nothing is as unusual as the Norman carvings. There is a curiously carved Jacobean pulpit with a considerable number of figures within arcades. There seems little to connect them. At each corner are vigorous figures, some of whom are praying. The thistle and rose indicates an early seventeenth-century date. The lectern is also unusual with its two carved figures. Are these women with moustaches or men with curiously large breasts?

Other features not to be missed include the stone effigy of a woman thought to be Lady Prendergast of Ludford. Her features have worn away over the last six to seven hundred years but her rosary beads are clearly defined. Interestingly, given the wear and tear, it was written in the early 1600s that the monument was then covered over by seats.

The Great War stained glass is also unusual in that it has a bi-plane as well as angels flying over France where Lieut. James Ponsford died. Note he is depicted

THE NORMAN
BEAKHEAD DOORWAY

THE CARVED PULPIT

as Saint George. There is also an unusually good slate memorial to seventeenth-century members of the Battishall family, two generations of whom served as vicars. Compare the mason's skill with that of another slate fixed to the porch.

Nearby see Abbots Bickington, one of the most charming churches in Devon. The small size of the building provides an intimate feel (which makes one highly-painted monument seem out of place) but the joy of the church lies in the four medieval panels of stained glass. The church's connection with Hartland Abbey may explain the high quality. Clockwise from bottom left can be seen St Christopher with the young Jesus, St Anthony with his pig and bell, the Trinity with Jesus as both child and adult along with a dove to represent the Holy Spirit, Christ crucified with a praying arch-bishop (notice the bands hanging from his mitre) or is it Abbot Gentian from Hartland Abbey?

⚷ *Open*

OPPOSITE: THE GREAT WAR MEMORIAL WINDOW

39
SOUTH MILTON

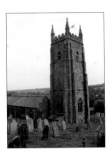

ALL SAINTS
POSTCODE: TQ7 3JW

This is one of the least assuming of all 50 churches in this collection. It is located in the heart of the South Hams and has a view of the sea. The church is not a grand affair (in the mid 1800s the Exeter Diocesan Architectural Society even dismissed its Norman door as 'neither very good nor early') but it has some intriguing aspects.

The font is the joy of All Saints although in 1841 it was described as 'a curious remnant of antiquity. It is a large rude and heavy stone basin'. The font dates back to the known origins of the building (to the 1100s) and has a series of puzzling figures.

A demon can be clearly seen (his ears are noticeably pointed) but less certain are what may be a man and a woman. Are they the parents of a baptised child? To their left might be a female tumbler, better known today as a contortionist. A similar one can be seen at St Marychurch. There are other figures, some of them animals, which cannot be easily identified partly due to some damage. These contribute to what is a highly unusual font for Devon. Even the EDAS commented on its 'grotesque figures'.

The painted reredos across from it is also unusual and described as 'a wretched modern painting' by one Victorian. This is from the eighteenth century and depicts Aaron and Moses. One angel is rather careless in her apparel and the cherubs are well-fed. It would have filled the east wall.

The rood screen is medieval with a curious mix of painting. The saints below, those that have survived, have a uniformity in their dress and faces. The birds above, no longer black if they once were, are keen to attend to their appetites. The parclose screen is also early as are the carved bosses and moulded ribs. These are

THE PAINTED WOODWORK OF THE
SCREEN WITH ONE OF THE BOSSES.
BELOW: THE SCREEN

TOP LEFT: THE EXTRAORDINARY FONT
TOP RIGHT: A STRODE RABBIT
BELOW: THE ANGEL FROM THE REREDOS

all roughly painted as if by a country workman. Needless to say the Victorian who regarded the font's carvings as rude and disliked the reredos felt the screen was 'gaudily painted'.

In the north chapel, around the organ, lie some floor slabs that were cut with considerable skill, in stark comparison to the early gravestones in the churchyard. That to Mathew Roope has three amenable armorial rabbits from the Strode family. Nearby: see Thurlestone, for an interesting collection of stained glass.

⚷ *Open*

40

SWIMBRIDGE

ST JAMES
POSTCODE: EX32 0PN

The exterior to St James is interesting: the sundial is eighteenth-century, the choice of an obelisk as a Great War memorial is atypical for Devon, the great fourteenth-century broach spire (like that at **Barnstaple**) is impressive and on the north side lies the grave to Parson Jack Russell, the illustrious hunting vicar who was at the church for 48 years. Swimbridge feels more remote than it is, not far from Barnstaple and yet on the edge of Exmoor.

In 1806 this was described as 'one of the neatest country churches in Devonshire' and there are three main items to see from just before the Reformation. The font is extraordinary: it stands some ten feet high and towers over any visitor with a canopy and possibly a reused sounding board from the pulpit. Two angels have held on to shields bereft of any heraldry or messages for untold generations. The font is a lead basin encased by an astonishing wooden structure (see Pilton) of three tiers with the canopy forming a fourth level. Was this put together after the Restoration by using existing sixteenth or seventeenth-century pieces of carving, possibly from benches? The Early Renaissance carving is extraordinarily fine, delicate and filled with eye-catching faces and some liberated angels.

The pulpit is a pre-Reformation treasure of carved stone like that at Dartmouth. It has saints (Paul, Peter, Augustine, Ambrose and Jerome) carved in each of the five facets. There is a satisfying richness to it and some original colours. Near it stands the wooden rood screen which again, in 1806, was commented upon as 'excellent carved wood work, painted and gilt, and in fine preservation'. It stretches 44 feet across the church in 11 bays. The carving is rich and enjoyable. In around 1830 the sections with the doors were taken down and stored. Fortunately they were not destroyed.

ABOVE: THE FONT ENCASED IN WOODWORK
OPPOSITE: THE HIGHLY CARVED SCREEN

AN EXHUBERANT FIGURE

DETAIL OF THE CARVING

The font, screen and pulpit dominate the church but there are also five pairs of pews at the rear of the nave which incorporate sixteenth-century carving. More early woodwork can be seen in the wagon roof particularly in the north chapel where there are a number of bosses which Miss Cresswell deplored as monstrous a hundred years ago. Fantastic coloured angels and double-headed figures can be spotted. These were painted and restored in 1727. The capitals on the columns also feature angels and a figure holding what may be a gridiron.

There are some notable monuments including one to John Rosier with possibly the least accomplished repainting of a figure (the two women look like milk chocolate). The excellent painted portrait of the dandyish Charles Cutcliffe on copper in the north chapel makes up for it.

🔑 *Open*

41

TAMERTON FOLIOT

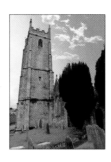

ST MARY

POSTCODE: PL5 4NB

The encroachment of Plymouth has gradually blurred the distinctiveness of Tamerton Foliot and it takes a bit of work to wind one's way through to the church. It does not have the presence of **Ottery St Mary** or **Cullompton** but has the charm of a once rural church.

The earliest item of note is a late medieval tomb chest to a knight and lady long thought to be members of the Gorges family (a descendant later came to control all of New England). Seven hundred years have left their marks on these two worthies but they are remarkable effigies. Two angels are still able to look to heaven and a few of their delicate hands have survived. Lady Gorges, if that is who she is, continues to wear a cross around her neck and the dog at her feet looks mournful if not worried.

The nearby early seventeenth-century monument to Sir John and Lady Susannah Copplestone is well done with nice emblems of mortality including a skull resting at Sir John's feet to indicate death. A pelican feeds her young above the prayer desk. Notice the two infants in their cots on either side; one of their heads rests on crossed bones but the other's has a flower with a death's-head on a petal. It is not obvious why Lady Susannah has she such a broad smile, perhaps its her jewelled cap. The female allegorical figures are top-heavy in more ways than one.

Of some considerable historical interest is the monument opposite of a shrouded female member of the Calmady family and possibly her two sisters. Is the main figure, set within scalloped shell, about to rise from the dead? The quality of the carving is high but the dusty colours and dark corner obscure the excellence of the work. It is comparable with the monument to Jane Fowell, also shrouded, in a corner of another church (**Plymouth St Andrew**).

COPPLESTONE BAMPFYLDE, A GREAT WAR MEMORIAL AND ONE OF THE
COPPLESTONE'S ALLEGORICAL FIGURES

The fourth notable monument is that to Copplestone
Bampfylde who died in 1669. This teenager rests with his elbow on
a skull but is depicted not at prayer but with his books and a quill
pen. The lines in Greek have been taken from the Andromache of
Euripides. There is a coarseness to the boy's face which is not due
completely to vandalism of his nose or to the flaring nostrils.

There are a considerable number of fifteenth-century bosses
in the roof. Some are replacements after a recent fire and a
goodly number are green(ish) men.

The font is fifteenth century but the later pulpit is more
interesting: it has some good carving and the angels share the
same distinctive compressed carving around their noses and
mouths with that of an angel decorating William Hearn's 1766 gravestone in the
churchyard. Along the base was written from Romans 10:14 'How shall they hear
without a preacher: How preach unsent: How shall they believe in him of whom
they have not heard'. A two-headed bird (an eagle? similar to one at **Alwington**) is
almost hidden as is the demonic figure to its right.

One stained glass window is unusual in that it depicts an African in chains
(like that at Bishops' Tawton) and the reredos in the north chapel has unusual
carvings (along the side) of emblems of the second world war including gas masks
and a stirrup pump. If any war memorial can be described as lovely then it is that
to Lieut. George Radcliffe. St George's dragon radiates beauty.

🗝 *Open by arrangement*

164   DEVON'S FIFTY BEST CHURCHES

42

TAVISTOCK

ST EUSTACE
POSTCODE: PL19 0BU

Part of the joy of Tavistock church is its setting, located within the ancient abbey precincts and the centuries-old market town. Modern Tavistock remains one of Devon's great market towns and Friday morning is a memorable experience.

St Eustace has been eclipsed by the town's two owners; it was in the shadow of the Benedictine Abbey from 974 until 1549 when the Duke of Bedford acquired the abbey and its land and then his family continued to dominate the town through to the mid 1900s.

The church was probably built in the early 1200s but was rebuilt and enlarged in the 1300s and 1400s. The notable feature of this period is the 'Clothmakers' Aisle'. This second south aisle was built in 1445 by Constance Wise, a local widow, and has its equivalent building from the cloth trade in the churches at Cullompton and Tiverton. The bones of Ordulph, founder of the Abbey, have been thought to be interred in the church and the base of the tower formed one of the abbey's gateways.

There are two noteworthy monuments. Along the north east wall is that to John Fitz and his family. He was, according to Reverend Prince in about 1700, interested in astrology and sought the most propitious time for his child's birth. Fitz asked the midwife to delay the birth by an hour otherwise he thought the child would come to an unhappy end. The midwife was unable to do as requested and a son was born. John Fitz died before his son, also called John, accidentally killed a man in a sword fight. The younger Fitz was pardoned by Queen Elizabeth but years later mistakenly thought he was being attacked in the night and killed a publican. He then stabbed himself and died of his wounds.

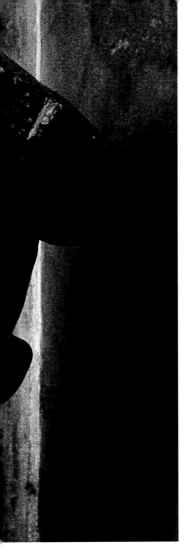

The more impressive monument is on the south east wall. This was erected to the memory of John Glanville, a prominent lawyer and judge under Queen Elizabeth. Some 200 years ago a local woman told at least one visitor that the judge's eyes were thought to move. More than 100 years before, in the 1690s, it had also been said that the liveliness of the carving fooled some visitors into thinking that the judge was a living person. Glanville died in 1600 and rests on his side while below him kneels his wife and five of their children. The latter were decapitated by the 1790s. The carver depicted the judge with a rather full face and this is interesting to contemplate given he died falling off his horse allegedly because of the 'unwieldy' weight of his body.

The church was restored in the 1840s and there is some extraordinary later glass. In the eastern window in the north aisle are depictions of the evangelists, prophets and Christ's life. These were designed by Burne Jones and the William Morris studio in 1875. Some of these figures were later replicated in churches across the country. The faces and colours are exceptional: there is a dream-like quality which at the same time is sensual and other-worldly. Morris had a financial connection with Tavistock through the Great Consuls Mine and the window is dedicated to a family relation. Also in the North Aisle is a window by Kempe. Here some figures are debased of their humanity. Two in particular could easily represent two Tavistock Victorians known as Barnicott's Ghost and Mat Martin. These two were familiar street characters eking out cheerless and melancholy lives. The former, a shrunken form waving a staff, shuffled along appealing for alms, and the latter only sought drink 'without which life was but a dreary blank'. They were, it was said at the time, better known than valued. Their faces could easily be those in the window.

Repositioned along the exterior of the church is a collection of notable slate gravestones which were the work of local masons. From amidst these stones there are views of the precinct of the abbey; of when the church would have been encased by ecclesiastical buildings and life.

⚷ *Open*

TOP: SIR JOHN GLANVILLE
BELOW LEFT: A FIGURE BY BURNE JONES
BELOW RIGHT: TWO DESPERATE FIGURES IN THE KEMPE GLASS

43

TAWSTOCK

ST PETER

POSTCODE: EX31 3HZ

Only Exeter Cathedral exceeds the 'Westminster Abbey of Devon' for its monuments. Before one arrives at St Peter's the lane passes the great Elizabethan gatehouse through which visitors travelled to Tawstock Court. The Bourchiers, created Earls of Bath in the sixteenth century, looked through their formal gardens to the parish church below. In the early 1800s St Peter's was described as 'the most curious church in the county' and this is all due to the Bourchiers.

Above the porch is a sundial by John Berry, dated 1757, which not only notes Tawstock time but that in such places as Jerusalem, Boston, Port Royal and Vienna. Along the south wall of the churchyard is the extraordinary gravestone to Philip Tamlin. The Resurrection Angel has a contorted body with sagging breasts but the detail of his hands with their fingernails is particularly unusual.

St Peter's has smiling faces on the fourteenth-century capitals in the nave and sixteenth and seventeenth-century benches scattered throughout the church. The most significant one is for the Bourchiers and is possibly pre-Elizabethan. This lies in the north transept and while modest in size it is finely worked. The woodwork seen high above is from a former gallery and in both transepts can be seen delicate eighteenth-century plaster-work in the ceilings. There are two screens: both the rood and parclose screens are early, unusual and detailed. Of the latter notice the roundels where one woman in particular has a head like an alien creature. The pulpit includes early woodwork but its distinguishing feature is a metal arm for an hourglass (see **Pilton**). The font has an elaborate cover with earlier detail.

These would all be of interest in any church but St Peter's great prize are the monuments noted as 'remarkable' as long ago as 1806. In the north transept is a

A RESURRECTION ANGEL OF THE EARLY NINETEENTH CENTURY

BON TEMPS VIENDRA

ABOVE: FRANCES, LADY FITZWARREN
OPPOSITE: ONE OF THE BOURCHIER'S TOMBS

chest tomb moved from Cornwall less than 100 years ago. Notice death strikes Sir John Wrey with a dart. Numerous monuments were erected to the Bourchier's staff and relations. Thomas and Anne Hinson have prayed towards one another for nearly 400 years as has William Skippon.

These are all fine monuments but the principal memorials are the ostentatious creations erected by the Bourchiers. The earliest is along the south wall in the chancel. Frances, Lady Fitzwarren, has lain on her six poster bed since the Armada. Her pose is, more than most, akin to Sleeping Beauty. It was created by her son William who intended to glorify the Bourchiers in general and himself in

particular. His text makes no reference to his mother's remarriage but does refer to malice and spite about her. The monument reminded the parish, his servants and guests of the lineage of the Bourchiers.

A generation later his monument was erected opposite his mother. This is also extraordinary work. He lies in state with his wife Elizabeth while their son and grandson kneel at one end and their daughter-in-law is at the other with her infant. The carving is rich, the alabaster fine and the impact just what William wanted. Notice the curious creature clutched by his son.

There are two other monuments of equal interest. Standing over them is Rachel Countess of Bath or she would be had the sculptor not supplied a copy of an existing statue of the Countess of Shrewsbury. Her husband is remembered to her left: the fifth earl of Bath has a monument presumably erected by Lady Rachel. Lord Henry was a Royalist and had been imprisoned in the Tower of London but was released during the war and lived out his days at Tawstock. Their monuments forego religious imagery. Lady Rachel's memorial also lacks colour and yet her life has detailed documents ranging from weekly gambling losses to feeding Prince Charles mazards.

Here is an opportunity to revel in monuments, they fill the walls but also the floors which have highly-carved floor slabs but it is too easy to be mesmerised by those at eye level and pass unobservant over those underfoot. The vast household of Tawstock Court stretch back generations silently waiting to be noticed.

⚷── *Open*

OPPOSITE: THE YOUNG EARL AND HIS SON, KNEELING BY HIS FATHER'S MONUMENT
RIGHT: ONE OF THE FOURTEENTH CENTURY FACES

LADY ELIZABETH.

44

TEIGNRACE

ST PETER & ST PAUL
POSTCODE: TQ12 6QP

Τhere cannot be a prettier church in Devon. The approach is unusual with a long drive but the exterior merely indicates how atypical it is: the windows have wooden frames except for the apse and there is no west door but access is through the tower which once had a wooden spire. It is only when one is inside that it becomes apparent that this is a church of elegant Georgian taste. Even so, in 1846 one writer summarised the church as having 'no pretensions to architectural beauty or uniformity in style'.

A century ago Miss Cresswell thought the interior 'was remarkable rather than ecclesiastical'. The walls are painted powder blue and the considerable number of high quality white marble wall monuments are shown off to their best advantage. As befitting a church of such prettiness, this is all sweetness and light. The brightness of the space, the blue of the walls and the white of the marbled monuments give it a feeling of refinedness and gentility.

In 1787 the Templar family at Stover demolished the existing church in order to completely rebuild. Through their new church the family publicly demonstrated their refined tastes but the villagers who attended Sunday service were mostly labourers and clay-cutters, possibly not the most receptive audience for Georgian elegance. The exterior owes much to the Gothic Revival and could usefully be described as Strawberry Hill Gothic but the interior is surprising. The centre of the building has a circular dome and there is internal symmetry: the chancel and transepts are of equal size. The pulpit originally stood along the north transept directly facing south where the Templar family had their pew.

The chancel of Teigngrace church

ABOVE: A TEARFUL ANGEL IN COADE STONE
BELOW: THE PIETA

Notice in the south aisle the cherub weeping for the two Templer sons who drowned in the early nineteenth century. He is made of Coade stone as is the monument to Nelson. Fame, one hand missing, rises above the globe with the text 'slain in battle'. On the north wall is an odd memorial to Charles Templer and depicts the loss of his ship, the East Indian *Halswell*, at East Man (named after the wreck) in Dorset in 1786. A dozen men are depicted attempting to clamber onshore. Above the apse is a large painting of the Pieta which has been attributed to James Barry although a Victorian writer identified it as West's 'Descent from the Cross'.

These memorials speak of pain, loss and bereavement and yet they contribute to the overall effect of appealing sweetness but in a very Georgian way.

⚷— *Open by arrangement*

45

TIVERTON

ST PETER

POSTCODE: EX16 6NW

In 1598 one 'poor beggarly' woman was frying pancakes when a spark ignited the thatch on her house. Fire spread through the town and then quickly consumed it. The town burnt down several times afterwards with the result that many of Tiverton's buildings are from the Georgian period onwards with only a few notable exceptions. St Peter's is one of them. It is, advised Thomas Westcote in 1630, 'worth your view'.

The church is a grand affair as one would expect from one of Devon's most prosperous market towns. There is much in the church but its most striking feature is the exterior of the Greenway Chapel which lies on the south side. Here one can see the ships which brought Tiverton's cloth to France, the Netherlands, Spain and France. It was that wealth that made the town's merchants so affluent and which made this chapel possible.

The chapel's white stone is in stark contrast to the red tower. The chapel and porch were built in 1517 and the latter had a Victorian rebuild. Other carvings are original including the scenes of Christ's life, only nine inches by eleven, some thirty feet above the visitor. Those of the ships are not unique (see **Cullompton**) but are nevertheless breathtakingly good, even those which have been recently restored.

The inside of the porch is remarkable. John Greenway was not reluctant to let future generations know who paid for this embellishment and his initials can be found in the stonework along with his effigy, and that of his wife, in the tympanum. They have been praying for nearly five hundred years at the Assumption of the Virgin. Few merchants can have achieved so much. There is a range of subjects depicted in stone inside the porch including ships, anchors,

The interior of the south porch

SOME OF GREENWAY'S SHIPS

the arms of the Drapers' Company and of the Merchant Adventurers, barrels, his merchant mark and even two-headed sea snakes. Part of the inscription reads:

> *While we think well, and think to amend,*
> *Time passeth away, and death is the end.*

The chapel itself is reminiscent of **Cullompton** but not nearly as grand. Even so the stonework is extraordinary and there are two surviving brasses of the Greenways which are easy to miss as they look like reproductions.

The rest of the church is radically different. The Victorians added a north aisle (see the exuberant gargoyles outside) and the only feature reminiscent of the Greenway chapel are two tomb chests in the chancel. Notice the carved faces on John Walrond's monument of 1579.

Other features not to be missed include the stained glass by both local and national makers and the Great War reredos in the north aisle which has particularly good carving by Herbert Read with details of the airman's goggles and the nurse with her bandages. The civic seats include what may be a seventeenth-century lion and unicorn. The painting of the Three Magi by Gaspar de Crayer is overwhelmingly large but is the black king merely delighted or surprised as well? Outside is what appears to be an early font, weathering in the elements.

⚷ *Open*

46

TORBRYAN

HOLY TRINITY
POSTCODE: TQ12 5UR

I n 1846 one local man wrote 'this rustic and secluded village may boast of a very handsome old church'. More than one hundred and fifty years later this fifteenth-century building remains simple, elegant and restrained as well as handsome. The church is in the care of the Churches Conservation Trust.

The lime-washed exterior, gleaming on a bright summer's day, is matched by a plain white interior but the joy inside is that it remains as it was before the Victorian improvements which happened elsewhere. Like **Parracombe** it illustrates a point in history, a medieval church which adapted to later changes but not overwhelmed by it. Before entering notice that the tower has a central stair turret and that the porch not only has stone seats but a graceful white-limestone fan-vault with four angels. It has a long wagon roof which must be later but was sensitively done. Eight and a half rows of Georgian box pews (made of oak?) lie along either side of the aisle but closer inspection shows that these incorporate fifteenth-century benches. The font is the same date as the benches: it is octagonal with an early seventeenth-century cover.

The medieval wooden rood screen is the joy of the church. It reaches across both nave and aisles and there are parclose screens of different designs. The painted figures on the rood screen are nearly complete. Some share very similar facial constructions. One of the unusual figures is St Victor of Marseilles who is depicted with his windmill.

The altar comprises the former pulpit and the seven-sided pulpit was made from parts of the rood screen. Bligh Bond, the expert on screens, thought the altar was a great treasure but regarded the pulpit as 'disproportionate and eccentric'

THE SCREEN

while Miss Cresswell concluded it combined 'an air of antiquity with considerable ugliness and true Gothic work is rarely ugly'. The candle sticks on the altar are thought to have been made from the Georgian altar rail supports.

Easily missed is the medieval stained glass in the heads of many windows. The lower nave angels are Victorian but above them are medallions with medieval angels and images of the passion amongst other designs. At the top of the East Window there are ten saints, some medieval. The modern glass is striking but discordant with the rest of the church. It is also unusual in depicting a boy scout although **Colyton** has one as well. The glass was inserted in 1931 as a memorial to Brigadier General Kelly. It depicts St George (as patron of soldiers), St Barbara (as patron of artillery and engineers), St Wolston (as patron of agriculture) and St Nicholas (as patron of seafarers and patron of boy scouts). The two latter saints were chosen to represent the general's retirement interests. The boy scout was dressed in Denbury's colours.

There is a rustic seventeenth-century floor slab to William Petter. It notes:

> *'Here under lies my corps*
> *Till god shall call*
> *From out this bed*
> *To judgment General'*

It is decorated not only with a heart pierced by arrows and a skull, crossed bones and hourglass but also a dancing figure of death who has a skull for a head (but a body of flesh) and carries an arrow and possibly a lantern.

DETAILS FROM THE SCREEN

⚷ *Open*

47

TORQUAY

ST JOHN THE EVANGELIST
POSTCODE: TQ1 1TY

In the 1850s the Anglican authorities in the burgeoning resort of Torquay decided to replace their ancient parish church of Tormohun. The medieval population along the bay had been low and those living in Tormohun were then easily accommodated in the small church. By the 1850s Torquay had become one of England's principal resorts and the Victorian period saw a considerable number of new Anglican churches. St John's was elevated from a chapel to being the principal parish church. A congregation had been meeting in a Georgian chapel but this was demolished and the chancel opened in 1864. Twenty-one years later the church was finished when the tower was completed.

Long before the tower was raised the church was High. George Edmund Street's design looms over the harbour but it has a dull exterior, like **Shaldon**, compared to the richness inside. The interior is lofty and the clerestory fills the church with light. This is a church set in the mid Victorian period. It does not have the surprises of fittings surviving from previous generations. Instead it presents itself as it was in the 1860s: Devon's leading centre of Anglo Catholicism.

There is a great deal of marble (some from nearby Petitor and also from Ashburton), brass and wrought iron; the pulpit is made of local marble. In the North Aisle there are mosaics by Antonio Salviati of the life of St John and the reredos is by Thomas Earp. There are copies of Burne Jones paintings on the north and south walls (the originals were recently sold). Most striking of all is the stained glass in the East Window by Morris & Company and the West Window by Burne Jones. The space at the east end is an immersion font (now railed in to stop parishioners from falling in?) and not far from it in the south lies Bishop Henry

Philpott's chair. Philpotts was a regular worshipper at St John's because one of his palaces was in Torquay. Nevertheless, he forbade the use of the sculptural reredos in 1864 and to satisfy him two plaster figures of the two thieves at the crucifixion were added. Philpotts withdrew his objections and after his death the two figures were removed. The vicar should have known to have tread carefully: nearly twenty years previously Philpotts had objected in the old building to two wooden crosses on the altar having floral decorations. He swept them from the altar with his stick. By the time of his death in 1869 the church was still being built and the rich embellishments we see today were slowly being added.

Open by arrangement

48

TOTNES

ST MARY

POSTCODE: TQ9 5RZ

The 120 foot tower is this church's best known feature. Thousands see it every day dominating the landscape and yet never step inside the church. The tower dates to the 1440s when the mason, Roger Growdon, toured local towers and chose Ashburton as the model.

There are three niches on the south side which are connected with the construction. In the centre is a mitred and bearded figure who has an inscription (*'I made this tore'*) and is thought to be Edmund Lacy, bishop of Exeter from 1420 to 1455. Two figures sit on either side, one may be Prior Stoke (who made a financial contribution in 1445) and the other possibly Thomas, Earl of Devon, who died in 1458. The tower is made of red sandstone from Stoke Gabriel.

The church extends partly over the site of the Benedictine Priory Church of St Mary which was demolished in order to build the new church comprising its nave (1432 to 1444), chancel (1445 to 1448) and tower (1449 to 1459). A north aisle was later added and helps to make this a substantial church. It is not as grandiose as **Ottery St Mary** or **Cullompton** but still impressive.

The remarkable interior feature is the stone rood screen which stretches across the church. The design is wonderfully variable and dates to about 1460. There are empty niches for statues. Early colouring can be found throughout the screen and one face and angel can be picked out. On the east side are some jolly figurative carvings, one creature is positively grinning. The parclose screen has, in the south chapel, carvings of friendly lions. The pulpit and font are also fifteenth century, the latter has a later cover with a gilded bird and the former was described in 1840 as having been painted to appear like mahogany. There were also 'devices of the 12 tribes of Israel in gay colours'.

At the entrance to the rood stairs

BLACKALL AND HIS FOUR WIVES

THE PULPIT WITH THE SCREEN
IN THE BACKGROUND

The elaborate entrance to the loft of the screen is located in the chancel and has a curious carving of what may be a cat or even a dog. Against the east wall once stood an eighteenth-century baldachin, a canopy which filled the space where the window had been.

For such a prosperous market town it is surprising that there are not more interesting and flamboyant monuments and indeed many have been removed since the early eighteenth century. Perhaps the baleful tone of the stone for William Yeo (*'my life was full of misery, of anguish, grief and pain'*) led to his being discarded. Walter Smith's sixteenth-century tomb chest rests in its niche and on the opposite side of the church is Christopher Blackall. He is marginally interesting; more intriguing is that the four women (Elizabeth Slanning who died in 1608, Penelope Hele in 1616, Susanna Halswell in 1622 and Dorothy Norris in 1634) below him are not daughters but wives. Unusually each woman was carved with individual distinctions. The Boer War memorial is also uncommon but that to the wayward John Prince is disappointingly staid. Perhaps the most interesting of all the church's monuments is that to Walter Venning who died of fever caught in a Czarist Russian prison. He was the founder of the Prison Society of Russia and is depicted along with a manacled prisoner.

The nineteenth-century stained glass is good and there are nice examples of the work of Fouracres of Plymouth. Also not to be missed outside the south porch is the town's Sword of Sacrifice on the Great War cross. This is the only sanctioned copy of Reginald Blomfield's design. Edward Windeatt, then mayor, worked tirelessly to erect the monument and then died hours before the unveiling. The sword thus represents not only the sacrifice of those who went to war but of Windeatt himself, arguably the town's leading historian.

Open

49
WEST OGWELL

WEST OGWELL CHURCH
POSTCODE: TQ12 6EW

first impressions are that this strangely difficult church to find is not merely rustically simple but perhaps too poor and uninviting. In 1793 it was described simply as being dark and damp. And yet this is a remarkable building: this is a church of about 1300. But it will take a discerning visitor to appreciate its fascinations. It not only escaped the improvements of the Victorian restorer but four centuries earlier it had not been given a Perpendicular makeover.

At the start of the nineteenth century the parish had 53 residents and only half that number were living there a hundred years later. Not surprisingly its rural position adds to an extraordinary sense of peace and quiet. This is helped by the lack of visual diversions, there are no bright colours to distract the eye. Box pews (painted white a century ago) fill the small space: there are a handful in the main body of the nave, some near the tower and a few more in the north transept where there are also curious arm rests for a child. The pulpit is from the seventeenth century, the font possibly of the eighteenth and the circular altar rails of the early nineteenth. The fittings are mere embellishments. The importance lies in the overall structure.

The plan of the building is important to understand: it was built in a cruciform form in the late 1200s with the tower added sometime between 1400 and 1600. The vestry is nineteenth century but there was no Victorian restoration.

What can be seen from its first building is the sedilia and the Decorated windows of the chancel and the north transept. In the south transept is a later medieval window but the two carved heads were reused and this window may have replaced an earlier one. The clear glass in the church is old.

The church is a reminder of what the Victorian improver was sometimes faced with. Fortunately it has been in the care of the Churches Conservation Trust since 1982.

🗝 *Open*

190

50

WINKLEIGH

ALL SAINTS
POSTCODE: EX19 8JF

All Saints is set in a large churchyard surrounded by thatched cottages within what has been until recently a compact village. In the early nineteenth century the church was best known for its associations with the writings of its extraordinary vicar, Reverend William Davy. Over the course of thirteen years he wrote *System of Divinity*, a collection of sermons which covered some 13,000 pages. He and a female servant did the printing and Davy sent a set, one of 14, to Bishop John Fisher but had no reply. Davy enquired if they had arrived safely and was told the bishop could not acknowledge every trifle that he received. He responded *'Well, my Lord, if you consider 26 volumes, the labour of fifty years in collecting, compiling and printing, a trifle, I certainly cannot allow myself to expect from your lordship either encouragement or support'*. At the age of 81 he became vicar at Winkleigh and six months later died after a life of what was termed anxiety and disappointment. Nearly fifty years after his death any gloom in the church was dispelled with an extraordinary restoration. This is a church for the Victorian enthusiast, for anyone who delights in colourful nineteenth-century decoration.

The church has medieval origins but its restoration in 1873 dominates the building. It was claimed at the time that All Saints 'from neglect and apathy it had fallen into a state of the utmost dilapidation and decay'. On a dark day a torch is necessary but even on a sunny summer's day the interior lighting is not strong enough to show the vibrancy of the decoration.

The walls have been enriched by sgraffito (from the Italian word sgraffiare meaning to scratch) and these take several different floral and geometric designs in bands of red or green. There are Minton tiles on the walls as well as the floors.

John Ford Gould, a Barnstaple architect, was responsible for the restoration. He commissioned Harry Hems to supply the wooden benches, a feature which few will notice because the walls and particularly the ceilings are so ornately decorated with considerable gilding. At the unveiling it was said the roof had 'golden colours'. Had Gould not died a few years later his legacy may be better known. This is the only church in Devon to house a bust of its restoration benefactor: near the tower can be seen a likeness of George Henry Pinckard, a local man who made his fortune in the insurance business. Members of his family contributed the pulpit, organ and clock.

Some thirty years later the chancel was restored. New choir stalls were put in, the roof was painted and Herbert Read carved the new oak screen.

Gould is also responsible for the extraordinary pulpit made of Derby alabaster and red Ogwell marble. Given its size, it is hard to imagine the pulpit had been in three locations in the church. It was intended to be placed where it is now but in 1871 the vicar situated it in the south aisle near the Gidley chapel and in 1915 the pulpit was moved further into the chapel. This resulted in Gidley family monuments being obscured and the family objected. In 1919 the pulpit was duly moved to where it should have stood originally and to where it remains today.

The church has an oddity on the exterior of the south transept. The Gidley chapel is thought to have been intended as a seventeenth-century mortuary chapel and at some unknown point a 'pumpkin head' was placed on the apex of the gable end. This is an unusual piece of sculpture and an unlikely gargoyle. Eyes, a nose and a grinning mouth with teeth have been carved on each of the three sides facing the public. Is it meant to be a death's-head? There is nothing like it in the rest of Devon. The more traditional angel standing over the east end gable is from 1873 but his near neighbour is a mystery. Above the south door the sundial notes:

> 'Life's but a shadow – man's but dust,
> This dyall sayes – dy all wee must'

⚷— *Open*

THE PUMPKIN HEAD AND DETAIL OF THE RICH VICTORIAN EMBELLISHMENT

SOURCES

The descriptions have all been informed by the Listed Buildings Surveys and the revision of Nikolaus Pevsner's *Devon* by Bridget Cherry. Each entry has also the benefit, when appropriate, of the work of antiquarians such as John Prince, Richard Polwhele and Samuel Lysons, as well as writers who were particularly interested in churches notably James Davidson, John Pike Jones, George Oliver, Stephen Glynne, Charles Worthy and Beatrix Cresswell. The publications of the Exeter Diocesan Architectural Society have been extensively consulted. Commentary on screens has inevitably involved consulting Frederick Bligh Bond and Dom Bede Camm, *Roodscreens and Roodlofts* (1909) as well as Bond's 'Devonshire Screens and Rood Lofts', parts one and two in the *Transactions of the Devonshire Association* for 1902 and 1903. More recent work that has been heavily relied upon includes John Scott, Frank Mack and James Clarke's *Towers and Bells of Devon*. In addition to these the following sources have been used to describe individual churches.

ALWINGTON

Theo Brown, 'The Folklore of Devon', *Folklore*, vol.75, no. 3 (Autumn 1964),
154 *A brief guide to the church of St Andrew Alwington Nr Bideford Devon*
Westcountry Studies Library, s726.5/DEV/DAV, James Davidson,
Church Notes West of Devon, 69
Ian Maxted, 'Richard Coffin', *Oxford Dictionary of National Biography*
(Oxford, 2004)

ASHTON

Marion Glasscoe, *Ashton Church Devon* (Ashton, 1993 edn)
Maxwell Adams, '*A Brief Account of Ashton Church and of some of the Chudleighs of Ashton*', Devonshire Association Transactions, 33 (1899), 185–98

George Oliver, *Ecclesiastical Antiquities of Devon and Cornwall* (Exeter, 1823), 138–9

Morris Drake, 'Heraldic Stained Glass in Ashton Church', *Exeter Diocesan Architectural and Archaeological Society Transactions*, 3rd series, II, 167–74

Westcountry Studies Library, s726.5/DEV/DAV, James Davidson, Church Notes South of Devon, 138

Westcountry Studies Library, Ashton parish folder, A5–8

Mary Wolffe, 'Sir George Chudleigh', *Oxford Dictionary of National Biography* (Oxford, 2004)

`The Restoration of Ashton Church Devon', *British Architect* (20 June 1902), 447

ATHERINGTON

Exeter Flying Post, 18 July 1877

Westcountry Studies Library, s726.5/DEV/DAV, James Davidson, Church Notes North of Devon, 317–20

BARNSTAPLE ST PETER

Barnstaple Parish Church (Barnstaple)

Westcountry Studies Library, s726.5/DEV/DAV, James Davidson, Church Notes North of Devon, 554

Mary Wollfe, 'George Peard', *Oxford Dictionary of National Biography* (Oxford, 2004)

BERE FERRERS

St Andrew's Church Bere Ferrers (1996 edn)

John A. Kempe (ed.), *Autobiography of Anna Elizabeth Bray* (1884), 164–6

E. I. Carlyle, rev. Deborah Graham-Vernon, 'Charles Alfred Stothard', *Oxford Dictionary of National Biography* (Oxford, 2004)

Westcountry Studies Library, s726.5/DEV/DAV, James Davidson, Church Notes West of Devon, 601

BICTON

Royal Cornwall Gazette, 1 February & 22 March 1850

Devon & Exeter Gazette, 25 July 1927

Todd Gray (ed.), *Travels in Georgian Devon* (Tiverton, 1998), II, 143

Peter Orlando Hutchinson, *A guide to the town and neighbourhood of Sidmouth* (1879), 97

Todd Gray, *Remarkable Women of Devon* (Exeter, 2009), 77–80

Saint Mary's Church, Bicton: a brief history

Westcountry Studies Library, s726.5/DEV/DAV, James Davidson, Church Notes East of Devon, 269–70

Devon Record Office, 1181A–2/PW5

Phoebe Stanton, *Pugin* (1971), 11, 170

BRANSCOMBE

Ronald Branscombe, *A guide to the church of Saint Winifred* (2004 edn)

Edith K. Prideaux, 'Branscombe Church, Devon', *Devon & Cornwall Notes & Queries*, 1912, 1–19

Todd Gray (ed,), *East Devon: The Travellers' Tales* (Exeter, 2000), 109

Francis Bickley, *Where Dorset Meets Devon* (1911), 233

BRENTOR

Charles K. Burton and Gerald Matthews, *The Church of Saint Michael, Brentor* (no date or place of publication)

Todd Gray (ed.), *Travels in Georgian Devon* (Tiverton, 1997), I, 122–3

Westcountry Studies Library, s726.5/DEV/DAV, James Davidson, Church Notes West of Devon, 545

Sabine Baring Gould, *Margery of Quether* (1891)

COLYTON

Francis Bickley, *Where Dorset Meets Devon* (1911), 170

W. H. Hamilton Rogers, *Memorials of the West, Historical and Descriptive* (Exeter, 1888), 97

The Parish Church of Saint Andrew Colyton

CREDITON

Vivian Summers, *Church of the Holy Cross Crediton* (Crediton, 2006)

Exeter Flying Post, 3 July 1889

Beatrix Cresswell, *Notes on Devon Churches, Deanery of Cadbury*, 38–9

CULLOMPTON

Eleanora Carus-Wilson, 'The Significance of the Secular Sculptures in the Lane Chapel, Cullompton', *Medieval Archaeology*, 1, 1957

Rosalind Northcote, *Devon, its moorlands, streams and coasts* (1930), 27

Todd Gray (ed.), *Travels in Georgian Devon* (Tiverton, 2000), IV, 188

Westcountry Studies Library, s726.5/DEV/DAV, James Davidson, Church Notes East of Devon, 417–29

DARTMOUTH ST SAVIOUR

Percy Russell, *Dartmouth* (1950)

St Saviour's Church (Dartmouth, no date given)

Westcountry Studies Library, s726.5/DEV/DAV, James Davidson, Church Notes South of Devon, 699

DODDISCOMBSLEIGH

Chris Brooks and David Evans, *The Great East Window of Exeter Cathedral* (Exeter, 1988), 43, 107–109, 113, 115, 118, 132

Exeter Flying Post, 1 October 1879

Keith Beer, *St Michaels's Church Doddiscombsleigh* (Doddiscombsleigh, 2004)

London Society, Vol. 49, 1886, 91

Westcountry Studies Library, s726.5/DEV/DAV, James Davidson, Church Notes South of Devon, 133–4

Westcountry Studies Library, S726.5/DEV/NOR, Devon Churches in 1830, 97

David Evans, Rachel Thomas and Roger Rosewell, *'Medieval and Modern'*, *Vidiumus* (online journal, accessed 4 September 2011), issue 10

EAST BUDLEIGH

Lillian Sheppard, *All Saints, East Budleigh, A Guide to the Church* (1978)

All Saints Church and the Village of East Budleigh (2010)

T.N. Brushford, 'The Church of All Saints, East Budleigh', Part 1, *Devonshire Association Transactions*, 23 (1891), 234–305; and Part 2, 26 (1894), 288–90

Todd Gray (ed.), *East Devon; the travellers' tales* (Exeter, 2000), 174

EGGESFORD

Friends of Eggesford *All Saints Trust, All Saints Eggesford* (Eggesford, 1992 edn)

Westcountry Studies Library, s726.5/DEV/DAV, James Davidson, Church Notes North of Devon, 179–83

ERMINGTON

The parish church of St Peter and St Paul Ermington Devon (no date, Ermington)

Edmund Sedding, 'Ermington Church', *Transactions of the Exeter Diocesan Architectural and Archaeological Society*, 3rd series, vol. 1, 1899, 56–9

F. Bligh Bond, 'Devonshire Screens and Rood Lofts, Part Two'. *Transactions of the Devonshire Association*, 1903, vol. 35, 456–7

William Cotton, 'On the churches of Cornwood, Harford and Ermington', *Transactions of the Exeter Diocesan Architectural and Archaeological Society* 3rd Series, vol. 6, 291–9

Westcountry Studies Library, s726.5/DEV/DAV, James Davidson, Church Notes South of Devon, 773

EXETER ST MARTIN

The Parish Church of St. Martin, Exeter (no date given)

J. G. M. Scott, *St Martin's Church, Exeter, Devon* (Churches Conservation Trust, 1998)

Robert Newton, *Eighteenth-century Exeter* (1984), 14–15, 30, 52–3, 55–6

Exeter Flying Post, 8 June 1826, 13 November 1856, 30 April 1879

George Oliver, *The History of the City of Exeter* (Exeter, 1884), 158

Haccombe

The Church of St Blaisie (Haccombe, 2001)
Westcountry Studies Library, s726.5/DEV/DAV, James Davidson,
  Church Notes South of Devon, 393–4

Hartland

Stephen J. Hobbs, *St Nectan's: the question of a seat* (Hartland, 2005)
Rosalind Northcote, *Devon, its moorlands, streams and coasts* (1930), 218
C. E. Byles, *The Life and Letters of R. S. Hawker* (New York, 1906), 54
Ivon L. Gregory (ed.), *Hartland Church Accounts, 1597–1706* (1950)

Hawkchurch

History & Guide St John the Baptist Hawkchurch Devon (Hawkchurch, 2010)
`Parish Churches, No. IX, Hawk Church, Dorset', *The British Magazine*,
  Dec 1832, II, 459–60
James Rudge, 'Letter from a Country Clergyman', *The Mirror Monthly
  Magazine*, 18 March 1837, 166–18

High Bickington

E.J. Winter, *St Mary's Church High Bickington, a brief history and
  guide* (1984)
Westcountry Studies Library, s726.5/DEV/DAV, James Davidson,
  Church Notes North of Devon, 265–6

Holcombe Rogus

Andrew Gabriel and Barbara Fletcher, *A Short History of Holcombe Regis* (1986)
Todd Gray (ed.), *Travels in Georgian Devon* (Tiverton, 2000), IV, 199
Westcountry Studies Library, s726.5/DEV/DAV, James Davidson,
  Church Notes East of Devon, 1–13
E. J. Barton, *A short history of All Saint's Church, Holcombe Rogus, Devon*
  (Holcombe Rogus, 1933), 1

Holne

Church of St Mary the Virgin Holne: a brief guide and history (Holne)
Fanny Kingsley, *Charles Kingsley, his letters and memories of his life* (1921), 85–6

Ilfracombe

Allen T. Hussell, *North Devon Churches* (Barnstaple, 1909), 7
John Roles, *Of Demons, Dragons and Dogs: the Medieval Corbels of Holy Trinity*
(Ilfracombe, no date given)
Westcountry Studies Library, s726.5/DEV/DAV, James Davidson,
  Church Notes North of Devon, 686

KENTISBEARE

P. J. Murray, J. L. Goodhall & P. A. Godall, *The Parish Church of St Mary, Kentisbeare, Devon* (Kentisbeare, 1997 edn)

Sadru Bhanji, 'Brass robbing', *Devon & Cornwall Notes & Queries*, XXXVIII, Part II, Autumn 1997, 57–8

LEWTRENCHARD

Bickford H. C. Dickson, *The Parish Church St Peter, Lewtrenchard & The Rev. Sabine Baring-Gould* (no date or place of publication)

Westcountry Studies Library, s726.5/DEV/DAV, James Davidson, Church Notes West of Devon, 422

LITTLEHEMPSTON

John Stabb, *Some Old Devon Churches*, I, 83–4

B F Cresswell, *Notes on Devon Churches, Deanery of Totnes*, 84–97

Charles Worthy, *Devonshire Parishes* (1887), 78–9

Westcountry Studies Library, s726.5/DEV/DAV, James Davidson, Church Notes South of Devon, 569–70

Hugh de Quehen, 'William Bogan', *Oxford Dictionary of National Biography* (Oxford, 2004)

MORTEHOE

St Mary's Mortehoe

Westcountry Studies Library, s726.5/DEV/DAV, James Davidson, Church Notes North of Devon, 681

OTTERY ST MARY

John A. Whitham, *The Church of St. Mary of Ottery in the County of Devon* (Ottery St Mary, no date of publication)

Sidney William Cornish, *Short Notes on the History and Parish of Ottery St Mary, Devon* (1869), 10

PAIGNTON

G. M. Rushforth, 'The Kirkham Monument in Paignton Church, Devon', *Transactions of the Exeter Diocesan Architectural Society*, 3rd series, IV, 1927, 1–37

George Oliver, *Ecclesiastical Antiquities of Devon & Cornwall* (Exeter, 1828), 123

Arthur R. Day, *The Parish Church of St John the Baptist, Paignton* (2010 edn)

PARRACOMBE

Church of St Petrock, Parracombe Devon (Churches Conservation Trust, 2006 edn)
    The Times, 19 December 1877
Rosalind Northcote, *Devon, its moorlands, streams and coasts* (1930), 254

PLYMOUTH ST ANDREW

Jack Spence, *Plymouth Minster: A History of St Andrew's* (Plymouth, 2011)
A Walk around the Church of St. Andrew Plymouth (Plymouth)
Westcountry Studies Library, S726.5/DEV/NOR, Devon Churches in 1830, 154

PLYMPTON ST MARY

Joseph Chattaway, `Plympton St Mary, Devonshire', *The Gentleman's Magazine*
    (June, 1829), 512–14 & 'Description of Plympton Church', *The Gentleman's*
        Magazine (April, 1830)
William J. Coppard, 'Church of Plympton St Mary', *The Gentleman's Magazine*
    (December, 1831), 489–91
W. J. Coppard, 'On the church of St Mary, Plympton', *Transactions of the Exeter*
    Diocesan Society, vol. X, 1856, 22–39
Plymouth & West Devon Record Office, 273/336 & 273/463
John Ferris, 'Sir William Strode', *Dictionary of National Biography*
C. H. Firth, revised L. J. Reeves, 'William Strode', *Dictionary of National*
    Biography
Plymouth & West Devon Record Office, 273/336
Westcountry Studies Library, s726.5/DEV/DAV, James Davidson,
    Church Notes West of Devon, 941
John Burke, *A genealogical and heraldic history of the commoners of Great Britain*
    (1838), IV, 427
Douglas Richardson & Kimball Everingham, *Plantagent Ancestry* (2004), 257–8
A short guided tour to the parish church of Plympton St Mary

PLYMTREE

Tony Eames, *The Parish Church of St John the Baptist, Plymtree*
    (Plymtree, no date given)
Exeter Flying Post, 10 July 1850, 11 & 18 September 1856
James Gairdner, 'Henry VII, Prince Arthur and Cardinal Morton from a
    group representing the Adoration of the Three Kings on the chancel screen
    of Plymtree church in the county of Devon', *The Academy & Literature*
    (7 September 1878), 331
Westcountry Studies Library, Plymtree parish folder, AB66

SHALDON

Westcountry Studies Library, Shaldon parish folder
St Peter: the parish church of Shaldon

SOUTH MILTON

Westcountry Studies Library, s726.5/DEV/DAV, James Davidson, Church Notes South of Devon, 857–9

SWIMBRIDGE

A guide to the parish church of St James, Swimbridge (Swimbridge, 2006 edn)
Westcountry Studies Library, s726.5/DEV/DAV, James Davidson,
    Church Notes North of Devon, 433
Westcountry Studies Library, S726.5/DEV/NOR, Devon Churches in 1830, 180

TAMERTON FOLIOT

P. S. Bebbington, St Mary's Church, Tamerton Foliot (Callington, 1981)
A few items of interest to look out for at St Mary's Church, Tamerton Foliot

TAVISTOCK

Exeter Flying Post, 6 January 1875
John Roberts, 'Drake's Worthy Friend: John Fitz (c.1529 – 1589), *Devon & Cornwall Notes & Queries*, Spring 1996, XXXVII, Part IX, 300–303

TAWSTOCK

Todd Gray (ed.), *Devon Household Accounts, 1627–59; Part II, Henry fifth earl of Bath and Rachel, Countess of Bath, 1637–1655* (Devon & Cornwall Record Society, NS 39, 1996)
Charles G. Layley, *The Story of Tawstock Church* (Tawstock, 1981)

TEIGNGRACE

Noel Thomas Carrington, *The Teignmouth Guide* (Teignmouth, 1893)
Judy Jolliffe, *The History of St Peter and St Paul's Church, Teigngrace* (ms)

TIVERTON

Stuart Blaylock, 'A survey of Greenway's porch at St Peter's Church, Tiverton', *Proceedings of the Devon Archaeological Society*, 44, 1986, 85–105
    The true lamentable discourse of the burning of Tiverton (1598)
A. E. Welsford, John Greenway 1460–1529, *Merchant of Tiverton and London* (1984)

TORBRYAN

Church of the Holy Trinity Torbryan, Devon (Churches Conservation Trust)
Charles Worthy, *Ashburton and its Neighbourhood*, 155
Westcountry Studies Library, s726.5/DEV/DAV, James Davidson,
    Church Notes South of Devon, 421
Devon & Exeter Gazette, 16 September 1931

TORQUAY ST JOHN

R. J. E. Boggis, *History of St John's, Torquay* (1930)
Percy Russell, *A History of Torquay* (Torquay, 1960), 114–116, 175–6
Parish Church of St John the Apostle Torquay: a short guide to the church

TOTNES

Jill Drysdale, 'St Mary's Church', in *Totnes* (Exeter, 2003)
William Cotton, *A Graphic and Historical Sketch of the Antiquities of Totnes* (1850)
Westcountry Studies Library, s726.5/DEV/DAV, James Davidson,
    Church Notes South of Devon, 550

WEST OGWELL

West Ogwell Church, West Ogwell, Devon (Churches Conservation Trust, 2007)

WINKLEIGH

Charles Worthy, *The manor and church of Winkleigh in the county of Devon* (1876)
Exeter Flying Post, 29 October 1873
E. Mortimer, *Notes on Winkleigh Church* (Winkleigh, 1982)
Chris Brooks and Bruce Induni, 'The Sgraffito decoration of Colaton Raleigh
    church and its conservation', *Devon Buildings Group Newsletter*, VI,
    October 1988, 13–14
Westcountry Studies Library, Winkleigh parish folder, A22, account by
    `Marland', undated
Devon & Exeter Gazette, 8 October 1919
Thompson Cooper, rev. Ian Maxted, 'William Davy',
    Oxford Dictionary of National Biography (Oxford, 2004)

List of Illustrations

Cover Images:

Top first row from left, Ashton, Colyton, Brentor, Holne, Colyton; second row from left, Doddiscombsleigh, Holcombe Rogus; third row, Branscombe, Dartmouth St Saviour, Haccombe, Cullompton, Mortehoe; fourth row, Doddiscombsleigh, Dartmouth St Saviour, East Budleigh, East Budleigh, Bere Ferrers; bottom row, Colyton, Winkleigh, Paignton, Torbryan, Colyton.

Illustration Sources:

Pages 15 to 16, W. H. Hamilton Rogers, *The Ancient Sepulchral Effigies and Monumental and Memorial Sculpture of Devon* (Exeter, 1877), plates III, X, XI, V, XVI; pages 19, 21 & 22, Daniel and Samuel Lysons, *Magna Britannia* (1822), VI, cccxxvii, cccxxxix & cccxxix; page 24, W. H. Rogers, *The Ancient Sepulchral Effigies and Monumental and Memorial Sculpture of Devon*, 154; pages 26 to 27, Westcountry Studies Library P&D05509; page 41, bottom left image by Stuart Blaylock; page 58, Devon Record Office, Z19/9/5; page 101, top image by Stuart Blaylock and bottom by John Allan; page 176, bottom image by John Baker; page 183, Richard Parker. All remaining photographs by the author or from his collection.

INDEX

DEVON'S FIFTY BEST CHURCHES

INDEX